THE GRAVITY OF FALLING UPWARD

TWO FRIENDS, TWO PATHS: A TALE OF LIFE CHOICES

RAKESH RANJAN EKANT

Contents

1. The First Bell	1

2. The Perfect Report Card	6

3. Shadows Of The System	11

4. Dreams Under Siege	18

5. The Price Of Perfection	22

6. Crossroads Of Dreams	27

7. The Golden Cage	32

8. The Weight Of Expectations	38

9. The Rocky Road	43

10. The Web Of Security	48

11. First Step Of Courage	52

12. The Art Of Survival	56

13. The Cost Of Complacency	61

14. Crisis Of Identity	65

15. The Road Less Travelled	69

16. The Illusion Of Stability	73

17. The Fall	77

18. The Rise Of The Underdog	82

19. The Courage To Quit	87

20. The Breaking Point	91

21. A Leap Of Faith	95

22. Starting Anew	99

23. The Power Of Persistence	104

24. The Hollow Success	109

25. The Awakening	114

26. The Entrepreneurial Spirit	119

27. The Return Of The First Bencher	123

28. The Gravity Of Falling Upward	127

Contents

29. The Unlearning Process — 132

30. The Rebirth Of Creativity — 136

31. The Reunion — 141

32. Beyond The Comfort Zone — 145

33. Building The Future — 149

34. The Chains Of Success — 153

35. The Freedom To Fail — 157

36. The Ripple Effect — 161

37. The Fallacy Of Perfection — 165

38. The Call For Change — 169

39. The Meeting — 173

40. A New Dawn — 177

41. Epilogue: The Meaning Of Success — 181

CHAPTER ONE

The First Bell

It was a crisp April morning, the air filled with the scent of freshly polished floors and the quiet hum of excitement as a new academic year began at St. Mary's High School. The first bell echoed through the hallways, signalling the start of a year.

Aniket sat at the front of the classroom, his books neatly stacked, his uniform spotless, and his shoes shining as if they mirrored his determination. He adjusted his spectacles, his eyes already focused on the blackboard, anticipating the teacher's arrival. The embodiment of a model student, Aniket was calm and collected, already planning his day with precision.

At the back bench straight to Aniket, Sahil slouched in his seat, his uniform slightly wrinkled and his tie loosely knotted. His eyes wandered around the room, more interested in the chatter around him than in the textbook sitting idly on his desk. Recently transferred to the city and newly admitted to the tenth grade at St. Mary's, Sahil carried with him the reputation of an average student, unremarkable yet unbothered.

From the very beginning, it was clear: the two boys were opposites.

"Did you hear about the new science teacher?" one student whispered, catching Sahil's attention. Meanwhile, Aniket was already flipping through his science textbook, uninterested in idle gossip. For him, knowledge was far more compelling than small talk.

The class quieted as Miss Rao, their teacher, entered the room. Her presence, firm but kind, commanded attention. The students stood and greeted her in unison, "Good morning, Mam."

She acknowledged them with a nod, her eyes briefly meeting Aniket's and then Sahil's before moving to the front. "Let's start with introductions," she said, her voice calm and steady. "Stand up, say your name, and tell us what interests you most in school."

One by one, the students introduced themselves. When Aniket's turn came, he stood confidently. "My name is Aniket Mehta, and I love learning new things, especially in science and mathematics."

Miss Rao smiled approvingly. "Very good, Aniket. I'm sure you'll excel again this year."

When Sahil's turn arrived, he rose more reluctantly, shifting his weight. "I'm Sahil Sharma," he began, his voice less sure. "I like sports... and sometimes history."

A few students chuckled, but Miss Rao silenced them with a look. "Thank you, Sahil. Both are important. I hope you find many things to enjoy this year."

As introductions continued, Aniket's mind had already moved on, planning his study schedule for the week. Sahil, on the other hand, stared out the window, his thoughts drifting far from the classroom.

The bell for the first period rang, and the lessons began. Miss Rao's voice filled the room as she guided the class through a science chapter. Aniket, quick to raise his hand, answered every question with precision. Sahil, meanwhile, doodled absentmindedly on his notebook, only half-listening.

During the break, a group of boys crowded around Aniket's desk, asking about the homework. He explained patiently, earning their respect as the go-to for academic help.

At the back, Sahil leaned against the wall, watching the group but already itching to head outside. He wasn't uninterested in learning, but he absorbed information differently—through experience, not through books.

"Hey, Sahil," called a boy named Rohan. "Want to play cricket during lunch?"

Sahil's eyes brightened. "Definitely!" he replied, his earlier boredom disappearing at the thought of the game. The group headed out, their laughter echoing through the hallway.

Aniket, content with his books, stayed behind, preferring solitude. For him, the classroom was a place of discovery, and missing even a moment of learning was unthinkable.

As the lunch bell rang, students poured out of the classrooms. Aniket, lunchbox in hand, found a quiet corner of the playground, his eyes occasionally wandering to the cricket field where Sahil and his friends played. Sahil's laughter carried across the yard; his joy evident with each swing of the bat. It was a stark contrast to the quiet focus Aniket maintained.

"They are wasting his time," Aniket thought, though a small, unfamiliar twinge of curiosity tugged at him. How could someone be so carefree?

The day unfolded much the same way. Aniket answered every question, earning praise from the teachers, while Sahil drifted through the lessons, engaging only when something sparked his interest.

In the final period, a history class, Mr. Kapoor asked the students to discuss the Indus Valley Civilization. Aniket, as expected, gave a detailed, well-prepared response, earning nods of approval from the teacher.

But then, Sahil raised his hand—a rare occurrence. "Sir, I read somewhere that they had an advanced drainage system and public baths. Isn't it amazing how advanced they were?"

There was a collective murmur of surprise among the students as Sahil raised his hand, something he rarely did. He leaned forward, his voice gaining confidence as he spoke. "Sir, I've been thinking about the Indus Valley Civilization. We always talk about how advanced they were with their cities and drainage systems, but no one really focuses on how they must have thought beyond just survival. Imagine what it took to build a society that cared not just about living, but about living well—public baths, trade systems, even art. They weren't just trying to get by; they were trying to create something bigger, something lasting. They understood that a civilization was more than just bricks and roads—it was about the people and the way they interacted. Their innovation wasn't just practical, it was visionary. They must have understood the importance of community, trust, and structure in ways we overlook today."

The room fell into a hushed silence, the usual casual whispers now replaced by wide-eyed stares. Mr. Kapoor, taken aback by the depth of Sahil's observation, paused for a moment before smiling. "That's an excellent point, Sahil," he said, clearly impressed. "You've gone beyond what the textbook offers. Yes, the Indus Valley wasn't just about their infrastructure but about their vision of society. It's rare to hear someone consider that. Very well done."

Even Aniket, who usually commanded the classroom with his precise and well-rehearsed answers, felt a knot of envy twist in his stomach. Sahil's insight wasn't something one could find in textbooks—it was a fresh, creative perspective. While Aniket prided himself on knowing the facts, Sahil had grasped something deeper, something that went beyond memorization. For the first time, Aniket realized that knowledge wasn't just about facts and figures; it was about how you saw the world and connected the dots.

The class murmured their approval, with several students nodding in agreement. Sahil's expression shifted from uncertainty to pride as he noticed the surprised looks around him. He had, for once, said something that not only stood out but also made everyone—including the teachers—see the material in a new light.

Sahil's face lit up, a sense of pride swelling inside him. It was a small victory, but it felt significant. Aniket watched, his expression unreadable, feeling, for the first time, a sense of competition—something new and unsettling.

The school day ended, and the final bell rang. As the students packed their bags, there was a shared sense of relief and excitement for the days ahead. Aniket meticulously organized his books, his mind already on the assignments awaiting him. Sahil, on the other hand, shoved his belongings into his bag, eager to meet his friends outside.

As they left the school gates, their paths diverged. Aniket headed home to his carefully planned study schedule. Sahil raced to the local park, where a group of neighbourhood kids were already setting up for another cricket game.

"Hey, Sahil!" a boy called, waving a makeshift bat. "We're short a player. You in?"

Sahil grinned, dropping his bag on the grass. "Of course! Let's play!"

For the next hour, Sahil lost himself in the game, forgetting school and the future in the thrill of the moment. Meanwhile, Aniket sat at his desk, engrossed in his studies, mapping out a future he believed was clear and certain.

But life, as it often does, had other plans.

As the sun set, casting long shadows over the town, both boys prepared for the next day in their own ways. Aniket, diligent and precise, set his alarm early, determined to maintain his position at the top of the class. Sahil, exhausted but content, drifted off to sleep, his mind filled with thoughts of the next cricket match.

And so, the two boys, as different as night and day, continued their respective paths—Aniket, the studious first bencher, and Sahil, the back bencher with a heart full of curiosity and courage.

Neither of them knew it then, but their paths, though separate now, were destined to collide. Their choices, shaped by these early days, would lead them to places they could never have imagined.

The journey of Aniket and Sahil was only beginning.

CHAPTER TWO

The Perfect Report Card

The classroom buzzed with excitement as the final bell of the term rang, marking the end of exams. A collective sigh of relief swept through the students, knowing that the days ahead would be filled with rest and freedom. The thought of a few days of relaxation, with no homework or tests, was a welcome break from the usual routine.

Now, after the brief leave, the school had reopened. The energy was different—refreshed, yet with the familiar rhythm returning. The hallways were alive again with chatter, students sharing stories of their short break, reconnecting with friends, and settling back into the daily flow. The teachers, too, seemed revitalized, greeting students with smiles, ready to begin a new chapter of learning.

Aniket sat at his desk, fingers drumming lightly on the polished wood, his eyes fixed on the teacher's desk where the stack of report cards lay. Confidence radiated from him, knowing the hours he had poured into studying would soon pay off. His only concern was whether he would surpass ninety-five percent in every subject this time.

Around him, the room buzzed with nervous energy. Students whispered anxiously, some fidgeting, others biting their nails. Near the back, Sahil leaned casually in his chair, his hands deep in his pockets, his expression detached. He had a fair idea of what his report card would look like and wasn't eager to see it.

"Why bother with these report cards?" he muttered to himself, barely audible over the chatter. "We all know what they'll say."

Rohan, sitting beside him, chuckled dryly. "Because they need to remind us we're failures," he said, though his attempt at humour carried a trace of bitterness.

Sahil shrugged, turning to the window where sunlight spilled into the room. It was a beautiful day, and he couldn't help but think of everything he'd rather be doing than waiting for a report card that would only confirm what he already knew. "I don't get why we're judged by how well we memorize things. What about everything else?"

Rohan raised an eyebrow. "What do you mean?"

"You know," Sahil leaned forward, his eyes lighting up. "Like building things, solving real problems. When we made that treehouse last summer, it wasn't just hammering nails. We had to figure out the angles, the support beams. That was real learning."

Rohan nodded thoughtfully. "Yeah, but none of that shows up on a report card."

Sahil sighed. "Exactly."

Their conversation halted as Miss Rao entered the room. The murmurs fell silent, and all eyes turned toward her as she approached the front, holding the stack of report cards. Her expression was unreadable.

"Good morning, class," she began, her voice calm and composed. "Today, you'll receive your report cards for this term. I hope you all did your best."

Aniket sat up a little straighter, his eyes locked on the cards in her hands. His pulse quickened, knowing this was his moment—the reward for all the nights he'd sacrificed, the hours spent hunched over textbooks. He briefly glanced at Sahil, who seemed indifferent. A part of Aniket felt a flicker of superiority, convinced that hard work was the only path to success.

Miss Rao's voice rang out again. "These report cards reflect your academic performance, but remember, they're not the only measure of your abilities."

Sahil smirked at the comment, feeling the hollowness of her words. He knew, as did everyone else, that grades were what mattered most in this system.

Miss Rao began calling names, one by one, as students anxiously awaited their results. The room was tense, filled with the soft rustle of papers and occasional whispers.

"Aniket Mehta," she called.

Aniket stood with purpose, walking to the front. Taking the report card, he quickly scanned the numbers: ninety-eight in mathematics, ninety-six in science, ninety-seven in English. His lowest mark was a ninety-five in history. A smile tugged at his lips. It was exactly what he had hoped for.

"Well done, Aniket," Miss Rao said, her voice warm with approval. "Your hard work shows."

"Thank you, ma'am," Aniket replied, his tone polite yet brimming with pride. As he returned to his seat, he felt the eyes of his classmates on him—some admiring, others envious—but none surprised. Aniket was always at the top.

While Aniket basked in his success, Sahil shifted uneasily in his seat as the stack of report cards dwindled. He wasn't afraid of failure; he had accepted it long ago. But seeing it confirmed in writing always stung.

Finally, Miss Rao called his name. "Sahil Sharma."

With a deep breath, Sahil stood, walking slowly to the front. He took the card, his eyes avoiding the numbers. Returning to his seat, he opened it hesitantly, glancing at Rohan's curious face.

"Well? How bad is it?" Rohan asked, leaning over.

Sahil sighed and unfolded the report card. The numbers were a blur of red marks and low scores. Thirty-five in mathematics, forty in science, fifty in history. His highest score was ninety eight in physical education. He wasn't surprised, but the disappointment hit him all the same.

"Sahil, I'd like to speak with you after class," Miss Rao said, interrupting his thoughts.

A few students exchanged looks, but most were too engrossed in their own results to pay much attention. Aniket, however, glanced back at Sahil, feeling a flicker of confusion. He couldn't understand how someone could be so detached from something as important as grades.

The bell rang, and the room erupted into a mix of excitement and relief. Students gathered in groups, discussing their marks. Aniket was at the center of it, his friends congratulating him on his perfect scores. He accepted their praise modestly, though his eyes gleamed with satisfaction.

Meanwhile, Sahil lingered behind, waiting for the room to clear. Miss Rao gestured for him to come forward once the last student had left.

"Sahil," she began, her tone gentle, "I've noticed you're having trouble with your studies, but I also see that you have a lot of potential. You're bright in ways that don't always show up on a report card."

Sahil shrugged, staring at the floor. "I try, ma'am. It just doesn't make sense to me."

Miss Rao leaned back in her chair, thoughtful. "I know it can feel like the system is working against you. But there are many ways to learn. You just need to find what works for you."

Sahil glanced up, a glimmer of hope in his eyes. "You really think so?"

"Absolutely," she said, smiling softly. "I've seen the way you solve problems, how you fix things others can't. That's a form of intelligence, too. It just doesn't always show up in these numbers."

Sahil smiled, small but genuine. "Thanks, ma'am."

"But remember," Miss Rao added, "you still need to work on your studies. Don't give up on them. I'm here if you need help."

Sahil nodded, grateful but conflicted. He knew he wasn't dumb, yet the world seemed determined to make him feel that way.

As he left the classroom, Aniket was waiting outside, his report card in hand. Aniket gave him a small nod, both acknowledgment and curiosity flickering in his eyes.

"How did it go?" Aniket asked, his tone carefully neutral.

Sahil shrugged. "The usual. Bad grades, maybe next time."

Aniket hesitated. "If you want, I could help you study. We could go over some subjects together."

Sahil raised an eyebrow, surprised. "You want to help me?"

Aniket nodded earnestly. "Yeah, I thought it might help."

Sahil considered the offer but shook his head. "Thanks, but I'm not sure it would work. I'm just not cut out for this stuff."

Aniket frowned, frustration seeping into his voice. "But you're smart, Sahil. I've seen you solve problems no one else could. You just need to apply that to your studies."

Sahil offered a faint smile. "It's not the same. Books and exams... they don't click for me. But thanks for offering."

As Sahil walked away, Aniket watched, feeling an unexpected sense of helplessness. He couldn't understand why someone wouldn't strive for success. For him, life was about achieving goals, and failure simply wasn't an option.

But as he stood there, a small doubt crept in. Maybe there was more to life than perfect grades. Maybe, just maybe, there was something to be learned from Sahil, who saw the world through an entirely different lens.

The rest of the day passed quickly. Aniket's parents were overjoyed with his report card, showering him with praise. His father beamed with pride, while his mother bragged to relatives about his achievements. Aniket soaked in their approval, feeling fulfilled by their recognition.

Sahil, on the other hand, faced a different scene at home. His father frowned at his report card, clearly disappointed. "You're not even trying, Sahil. What is this?"

"I am trying, Dad," Sahil replied quietly. "I just... don't get it."

His father sighed; the frustration evident. "You need to work harder. Life's not a game."

His mother, softer in her approach, placed a hand on his father's arm. "Let's not push him too hard. He's doing his best."

Sahil nodded, though inside, he wasn't sure if he was doing his best or if his best would ever be enough. He felt trapped in a system that didn't value his skills, his way of learning.

That night, as he lay in bed, Miss Rao's words echoed in his mind. Maybe there was a way to find success, just not in the way everyone expected. And for the first time in a long while, he felt a spark of hope—perhaps, somewhere, there was a place for someone like him.

And so, the two boys, each walking their own path—Aniket, with his perfect report card and life; and Sahil, still searching for his place in a world that didn't seem to understand him—continued their journeys. But this was only the beginning, and the lessons ahead would be far more transformative than either of them could imagine.

CHAPTER THREE

Shadows of the System

The classroom was quiet, save for the rhythmic scraping of chalk on the blackboard. Miss Taneja hand moved swiftly, writing out the details of a complex mathematical equation. Occasionally, her gaze swept across the room, ensuring the students were following. Aniket sat at his desk, posture perfect, his eyes glued to the board with unwavering attention. His notebook was immaculate, each line meticulously copied. It was clear to anyone watching that he was in his element.

In the back row, Sahil was far less focused. His eyes wandered, and his pen tapped absently on the desk as the numbers on the board blurred before him. He tried to focus, but his thoughts drifted back to the cricket game he had played with friends the previous evening. The rush of adrenaline as he hit the ball for a six excited him far more than the lifeless symbols in front of him.

Miss Taneja paused, turning her attention to the class. "Aniket," she called, her voice breaking the silence. "Would you come up and solve the next problem?"

The class murmured in approval as Aniket stood, moving with quiet confidence. His shoes barely made a sound against the tiled floor as he reached for the chalk. With practiced ease, he completed the equation, his movements sure and precise.

"Well done, Aniket," Miss Taneja said with a trace of pride in her voice. "That's exactly right."

Aniket returned to his seat, a small smile playing on his lips. The familiar satisfaction of mastering a challenge washed over him. This was where he thrived, and he knew it.

Miss Taneja's gaze shifted to the back of the room. "Sahil," she said, her tone markedly less encouraging, "come up and try the next one."

Sahil stiffened, caught off guard. He hadn't expected to be called on, especially after his previous failed attempts. Hesitating, he felt the pounding in his chest intensify.

"Well?" Miss Taneja prompted, her patience thinning. "We're waiting."

A ripple of laughter passed through the class, and Sahil's face burned with embarrassment. Slowly, he stood, feeling the weight of the room's eyes on him. His legs felt heavy as he approached the board, his palms sweaty. He picked up the chalk, staring at the equation as if it were written in another language.

"Go ahead," Miss Taneja urged, though her tone carried more exasperation than encouragement.

Sahil's hand trembled as he scrawled a few tentative numbers on the board, his uncertainty evident. The class watched in uncomfortable silence, with some glancing at each other in amusement.

"That's not correct, Sahil," Miss Taneja said finally, her voice tinged with disappointment. "You need to pay more attention in class. This isn't the first time you've been distracted."

Sahil dropped the chalk, muttering an apology as he trudged back to his seat. His classmates began to whisper as soon as he sat down.

"Couldn't even solve that," someone muttered.

"Probably too busy daydreaming about cricket," another added, eliciting a few snickers.

Sahil clenched his fists under the desk, his face flushed with shame. He wanted to shout back, to explain that he wasn't stupid, that this simply wasn't his thing. But he knew it wouldn't matter. The label had already been slapped on him, and there was no shaking it off.

The rest of the lesson passed in a blur for him. Miss Taneja continued with the equations, calling on Aniket and a few others who answered her questions with ease. Sahil kept his head down, his mind elsewhere, far from the classroom and the taunting numbers on the board.

When the bell rang, signalling the end of the period, Sahil felt a wave of relief. He hurriedly gathered his things, eager to escape the judgmental eyes and whispered mockery. He made his way to the playground, the open space offering a sense of freedom he never felt within the confines of the classroom.

Aniket lingered behind, surrounded by a small group of students congratulating him on his performance. He accepted their praise with a polite smile, though his thoughts wandered to Sahil, who had quietly slipped out. Aniket felt a pang of confusion and pity. Sahil was smart in his own way, but he seemed indifferent to the things that mattered most.

"He should try harder," one of his classmates remarked. "These problems aren't that difficult."

Aniket nodded absently, his mind still on Sahil. "Yeah, maybe he just needs to focus more," he murmured, though the words felt hollow.

The day moved on, and as it did, Sahil found himself increasingly isolated. The incident in math class had only solidified his reputation as a student who didn't take his studies seriously. The teachers began to regard him with suspicion, their gazes filled with disappointment and frustration. Anytime he tried to ask a question or contribute, his efforts were met with skepticism.

During a science class, Mr. Singh was explaining the concept of electric circuits, drawing a simple diagram on the board. His voice carried over the classroom, detailing the basics.

"Electricity flows through conductors like metal," he said, tapping the diagram, "and is resisted by insulators, like rubber or plastic."

Sahil, who had been sitting at the back, lost in thought, suddenly felt a question bubble to the surface. Without thinking much, he raised his hand, surprising not only the teacher but also his classmates, who rarely saw Sahil this engaged.

Mr. Singh stopped, intrigued by the rare gesture. "Yes, Sahil?" he asked, curious to see what was on his mind.

Sahil hesitated, feeling the class's attention shift toward him. But his curiosity pushed him forward. "Sir, if we connected the circuit to something other than a light bulb—like a fan or a motor—would it still work?"

The question caused a slight murmur of confusion among the students. It wasn't the kind of question they were expecting, certainly not from someone like Sahil, who usually kept his head down. Aniket, always sharp and quick to grasp concepts, raised an eyebrow, trying to figure out where Sahil was going with this.

Mr. Singh, though, smiled, seeing where the question was headed. "Yes, Sahil. The circuit would work with a fan or a motor, but the amount of current needed might be different depending on the device. A motor, for example, might require more power than a light bulb."

Sahil's interest sparked. "So, if I wanted to use a small motor to power something, like a toy car, I'd need to change the circuit to give it more power, right?"

Mr. Singh nodded approvingly. "Exactly. You'd need to increase the power source or change the components in the circuit—like using a bigger battery or thicker wires to handle the extra current."

The class grew quieter as the conversation drifted slightly beyond the basic lesson, they had all prepared for. Some students glanced at each other, unsure of where the discussion was headed. Aniket, who usually excelled in these moments, found himself listening more intently than usual.

Sahil continued, encouraged by Mr. Singh's response. "But what if the motor needs more power to start than to keep running? How does the circuit handle that?"

Now, the conversation was going deeper, and the confusion among the students was palpable. Aniket's brow furrowed slightly as he tried to keep up with the thought process. This was no longer about just following what was written in the textbook.

Mr. Singh, though irritated with the direction of the discussion, composed and leaned against his desk. "Good observation, Sahil. Yes, some motors need more power to start than to keep running—this is called the starting current. In those cases, the circuit has to be designed to handle that initial surge, but once the motor is running, it will settle into needing less power. That's why some circuits use resistors or even switches to control that surge."

Sahil nodded, his mind working quickly. "So, if I wanted to build a project with a motor, I'd need to make sure the wires and the battery are strong enough to handle that starting current, right?"

"Yes, you would," Mr. Singh said. "It's a good thing you're thinking about how to adjust the circuit for different needs. It shows you're considering how electricity behaves in real-world applications."

Around the classroom, most students had fallen silent, some staring blankly, others doodling in their notebooks. This wasn't what they had signed up for. Aniket, normally the one driving the discussion forward, felt a twinge of surprise. He had always been the top student, but Sahil's line of thinking was unexpected and thoughtful in a way that went beyond simply memorizing facts.

Sahil, however, was lost in thought, envisioning the potential of his ideas. "So, if I tried to build something with a motor, like a small windmill or a toy car, I could make sure it works by checking the battery size and the wire thickness first?"

Mr. Singh's though irritated with the direction going beyond the syllabus smiled and said. "Exactly, Sahil. It sounds like you're ready to take on a project. That's the beauty of science—you apply the basics to create something entirely new. But, first try to focus on the syllabus."

The bell rang, signalling the end of the class, but Sahil's mind was still spinning with ideas. He had caught a glimpse of how the simple circuits they learned about could be turned into real projects.

As students packed up, whispers began to ripple through the room.

For the first time in what felt like ages, Sahil experienced a surge of validation. But the moment was brief as the teacher quickly reminded him to stay focused on the syllabus. Once again, Sahil felt trapped within the rigid framework society had built for him.

As the class ended, the whispers returned.

"Why does he care about motors?" one boy scoffed. "He can't even pass a test."

"Probably wants to build some silly toy," another voice added, followed by laughter.

The pride Sahil had felt dissolved, replaced by the familiar sting of ridicule. He clenched his jaw, frustration bubbling inside him. Why couldn't they see the world the way he did? Why did everything have to revolve around grades and exams?

The teachers, too, seemed to lose patience with him. They called on him less and less, their voices tinged with irritation whenever he tried to speak. It was as if they had already given up, decided that he wasn't worth their time.

Meanwhile, Aniket continued to excel. His name became synonymous with success. He topped every exam, answered every question with ease, and the teachers adored him. Every word from them was filled with praise.

"You're going to do great things, Aniket," Mr. Singh told him one afternoon after class. "You have a bright future ahead."

"Thank you, sir," Aniket replied, his voice humble but proud. As he walked out of the classroom, he glanced at the empty desk in the back where Sahil usually sat. Sahil had become more absent lately, slipping further into the background. Aniket couldn't understand it. Sahil had potential, but he didn't seem to care about the things that really mattered.

During recess, Aniket spotted Sahil sitting alone under a tree, his back against the bark, staring into the distance. After a moment of hesitation, Aniket walked over.

"Hey," he said awkwardly.

Sahil looked up, surprised. "Hey," he replied, his tone cautious.

"I heard what you said in science class," Aniket began, his voice uncertain. "About the motor. It was a good question."

Sahil shrugged; his expression guarded. "Thanks."

Aniket shifted his weight uncomfortably, searching for the right words. "You know, you're smart, Sahil. You think about things differently. It's just... the school doesn't always recognize that."

Sahil laughed, a humourless sound. "Yeah, I've noticed. It feels like the system only cares about one thing: memorizing facts and passing exams."

Aniket nodded slowly, a flicker of guilt tugging at him. He had never questioned the system because it had always worked for him. But Sahil's struggles made him wonder if the system itself was flawed.

"Maybe you just need to find a way to make it work for you," Aniket suggested.

Sahil glanced toward the playground, where their classmates gathered in groups, laughing and chatting. "I don't know, Aniket. It feels like once you get labelled in this system, there's no way out."

Aniket had no response. He knew Sahil was right. Once the teachers placed you in a box, it was almost impossible to escape.

The bell rang, signalling the end of recess, and the two boys stood, brushing the dust off their uniforms as they headed back to class in silence, each lost in their own thoughts.

As the days passed, the gap between Aniket and Sahil grew wider. Aniket continued to win every award and top every test. The system loved him, praised him as the model student. Sahil, on the other hand, slipped further into disillusionment. He began skipping classes, his presence increasingly unremarkable to the teachers, who had grown tired of his lack of interest.

One afternoon, after a particularly gruelling exam, Aniket found Sahil sitting alone on a bench in the playground, his face hidden in his hands. Hesitating for only a moment, Aniket sat beside him.

"You didn't show up for the exam today," Aniket said quietly.

Sahil looked up, his eyes red-rimmed. "What's the point? I wasn't going to pass anyway."

Frustration welled up inside Aniket. "You're smart, Sahil. You just need to try harder."

Sahil laughed bitterly. "Try harder? You don't get it, do you? I've been trying, Aniket. I've been trying so hard, but it's never enough."

Aniket fell silent. For the first time, he didn't have the answers. He didn't know how to help. All he could do was sit there, feeling the weight of the system pressing down on both, shaping them in ways neither fully understood.

As the sun dipped below the horizon, casting long shadows across the playground, Aniket made a silent vow. Somehow, he would find a way to help Sahil. He would make the system see what he saw: that Sahil was more than a troublemaker, more than a label.

But for now, all he could do was sit beside his friend, the two of them united in their isolation, unaware of the battles and choices that would shape their lives.

CHAPTER FOUR

Dreams Under Siege

The classroom buzzed with excitement as Miss Rao announced the new project. The task was simple: write an essay on your dream career and how you plan to achieve it. It was the kind of assignment that filled the room with hope and ambition, a glimpse into the futures the students envisioned for themselves.

Aniket's eyes sparkled as his pen moved swiftly across the page. His handwriting, neat and precise, filled the paper with a vision he had nurtured for as long as he could remember. He was going to become an engineer, a top-notch one, the kind who worked on groundbreaking technologies for prestigious companies. His path was clear: excellent grades, a scholarship to a renowned university, and then a coveted position at a multinational firm.

As he wrote, the future unfurled before him in vivid detail: modern offices with glass walls, intellectual discussions with like-minded colleagues, and the satisfaction of solving complex problems that would shape the world. His dream was carefully constructed, brick by brick, and he was determined to bring it to life.

In contrast, Sahil stared at his blank sheet of paper, the word "Dream" seeming to mock him. What was his dream? To escape, perhaps — to break free from the confines of school, this town, and the life that felt imposed upon him. His mind wandered to the world beyond the classroom: bustling cities, serene mountains, endless deserts. He wanted to experience life, to learn from the world itself, not just from textbooks and teachers who didn't understand him.

But how could he express that in words? How could he articulate a dream with no clear path, no structured plan like Aniket's? He glanced at his friend, who was already deep into his essay, his face glowing with purpose. Aniket knew what he wanted, and Sahil felt adrift in comparison — lost in a sea of vague possibilities.

"Is everything okay, Sahil?" Miss Rao's voice broke through his thoughts. She stood beside his desk; her eyes soft with concern as they rested on the empty page before him.

He forced a smile. "Yes, ma'am. I'm just thinking."

Her gaze softened further. "Take your time. This is your future we're talking about. It's important."

Her words lingered in the air like a challenge. *It's your future.* But what did that really mean? The future felt like an abstract concept — a distant collection of days, each one blending into the next. Sahil struggled to imagine himself ten or twenty years down the line. Where would he be? What would he be doing? No clear image formed in his mind, just a hazy vision of himself standing on the edge of a vast, empty field, the horizon forever out of reach.

Aniket, meanwhile, had completed his essay, filling the pages with purpose. Glancing over at Sahil, who was still staring at his blank paper, he felt a pang of concern. Sahil had so much potential, but he seemed unable to find direction. Aniket wanted to help, but he didn't know how.

As the class ended and students began to file out, Aniket approached him. "Do you want to talk about it? The essay, I mean."

Sahil looked up, surprised. "What's there to talk about? I don't even know what to write."

"Maybe you could start with what you enjoy," Aniket suggested. "What excites you."

Sahil let out a hollow laugh. "Excites me? I don't know if I'm excited about anything."

Aniket frowned, his voice tinged with frustration. "That's not true. You're great with your hands, building things. You're always curious about how things work. You could be an inventor or even an engineer."

"Like you?" Sahil's tone sharpened, his eyes narrowing. "No, Aniket. I'm not like you. I don't want to sit in an office solving problems that don't matter. I want to do something real, something meaningful."

Aniket recoiled slightly, stung by Sahil's words. "What's wrong with being an engineer? It's a respectable job. You can make a real difference."

Sahil shook his head, weariness creeping into his voice. "You don't get it. You've got everything planned, and that works for you. But I can't see myself living that kind of life."

Aniket fell silent, struggling to understand Sahil's resistance. He could see the frustration in his friend's eyes — the feeling of being trapped in a system that didn't value him for who he was.

"What *do* you want to do?" Aniket asked softly, genuinely curious. "If you could choose anything, what would it be?"

Sahil hesitated; his gaze distant. "I want to see the world," he said finally. "I want to travel, meet people, learn from them. I want to experience life, not just read about it."

Aniket blinked in surprise. "That's... amazing, Sahil. But how do you plan to make it happen?"

Sahil shrugged. "That's the problem, isn't it? Everyone tells me I need a plan. But what if I just want to live?"

Aniket didn't know how to respond. He had always believed in having goals, a clear path. But here was Sahil, challenging everything he had been taught to value.

"It's not that simple," Aniket said gently. "You need some kind of stability, something to fall back on. You can't just... wander."

"Why not?" Sahil's eyes flashed with intensity. "Why does everything have to be controlled? Why can't I just go where life takes me?"

"Because the world doesn't work that way," Aniket said, frustration seeping into his voice. "You have to take responsibility, make choices."

Sahil's expression hardened. "Maybe I don't want to live in your world, Aniket. Maybe I want to find my own."

Aniket stared at him, feeling an unfamiliar sense of distance between them. He wanted to argue, to convince Sahil that he was making a mistake, but he knew it would be pointless.

"I just don't want you to regret it," Aniket said quietly, almost pleading. "I don't want you to look back one day and feel like you wasted your potential."

Sahil's gaze softened. "I appreciate that, Aniket. But I have to live my own life. Even if it means making mistakes."

Aniket nodded slowly, though his heart weighed heavy. He didn't agree, but he couldn't force Sahil to see things his way. All he could do was hope his friend would find his path.

As they parted ways, the conversation lingered in Aniket's mind. For the first time, he felt a flicker of doubt. Had he been so focused on his future that he had forgotten to live in the present?

That night, as Aniket sat at his desk, textbooks spread before him, his thoughts kept drifting back to Sahil's words. "I want to experience life, not just read about it." The phrase echoed in his mind, stirring something deep inside him. Could there be more to life than following a carefully laid-out plan?

Meanwhile, in a cluttered room on the other side of town, Sahil lay awake, his mind racing. He felt trapped — by his parents' expectations, by his teachers, by society. Everyone wanted him to be something he wasn't. He thought about the essay he hadn't written, about the dream he couldn't fit into neat, expected boxes.

The next day, the essays were due. Aniket submitted his with a sense of accomplishment, the neatly written pages reflecting his hard work. In contrast, Sahil handed in a single, hastily scribbled sheet.

Miss Rao glanced at it, her brow furrowed as she read the brief, almost defiant sentences: *"I don't know what my dream is. I just want to find it on my own. I want to live my life, not someone else's version of it."*

She sighed, her heart aching for him. "Sahil, you have so much potential. But you need to find a way to channel that energy."

He shrugged. "Maybe I will. Maybe I won't. But I have to do it my way."

And so, the two boys, so different yet bound by their desire to find their place in the world, continued their journeys — Aniket with his meticulously planned future, and Sahil with his untamed dreams. Though their paths diverged, the weight of their aspirations lingered with them, shaping the choices they would make and the lives they would lead.

The Price of Perfection

The piercing sound of the alarm echoed in Aniket's bedroom, signalling the start of another day. He reached out mechanically to silence it, eyes blinking open as the first light of dawn filtered through the curtains. For a moment, he lay still, mentally ticking through his meticulously planned day: extra math practice before breakfast, reviewing the science project during breaks, and perfecting the history assignment. There was no room for error.

With a sigh, he pushed himself out of bed, glancing at the stack of books neatly arranged on his desk. Each one had its place, organized by subject, offering him a brief sense of satisfaction before the familiar weight of responsibility settled in. He couldn't falter—perfection was his only option.

Downstairs, his mother greeted him with a smile as she prepared breakfast. The smell of freshly brewed tea filled the kitchen. "Good morning, Aniket. Up early again? You're always working so hard."

He nodded, his eyes drifting toward the open textbook on the kitchen table. "Just revising, Mom. I need to stay ahead."

His mother placed a cup of tea in front of him, her voice filled with pride. "You're doing so well, beta. Your father and I are so proud. Keep it up, and you'll achieve everything you've ever dreamed of."

Aniket forced a smile as he sipped the tea. It was sweet, almost too sweet, but he didn't say anything. He knew how much his parents had sacrificed for his education, how much they expected from him. He couldn't afford to let them down. Perfection was the price.

At school, the day passed in a blur of classes, assignments, and never-ending expectations. Aniket answered every question flawlessly, his hand always the first to shoot up. The teachers' praise barely registered anymore; it felt hollow, like an echo of something that had once mattered but no longer did. The pressure was suffocating.

"Excellent work, Aniket," Mr. Singh said in math class after another correct answer. "You're setting the bar for everyone."

Aniket nodded politely; his smile tight. He felt the distance between himself and his classmates growing with each passing day. Admiration? Maybe. But also envy and detachment. He wasn't like them, and they knew it.

During lunch, he retreated to the library, books spread out before him. Outside, he could hear laughter, carefree voices drifting in through the open windows. Among them was Sahil's voice—loud, unburdened, and full of life. For a fleeting moment, Aniket envied him. Sahil never seemed to care about the pressures that weighed so heavily on Aniket's shoulders. He didn't seem to care about perfection.

He shook the thought away and refocused on his work. There was no time for distractions. He had to stay ahead.

Meanwhile, outside, Sahil was leaning against a tree, his hands stained with grease from the small motor he had salvaged. His shirt was dirty, but his eyes were bright with excitement as he tinkered with the motor, coaxing life into its rusted parts.

"Why do you bother with that stuff?" Rohan asked, amused. "It's not going to help you pass your exams."

Sahil shrugged, tightening a screw. "I enjoy it. Besides, who knows? I might learn something useful."

Rohan grinned. "You're a strange guy, Sahil."

Sahil laughed, wiping his hands on his already stained shirt. "Maybe. But at least I'm having fun."

The motor sputtered to life, its blades whirring softly. Sahil's grin widened, satisfaction washing over him. It wasn't much, just an old fan motor brought back to life, but it was his accomplishment.

"You're pretty good at this stuff," Rohan said, his tone now more admiring than teasing. "You could fix anything."

Sahil smiled, shrugging modestly. "Maybe. I just like figuring things out."

Rohan's expression grew serious. "But don't forget about studying. You can't just fix motors for the rest of your life."

Sahil sighed, the excitement fading slightly. "I know. But when I'm stuck in a classroom all day, I feel like I can't breathe. This is what makes me feel alive."

He glanced toward the library, catching sight of Aniket through the window. His friend sat alone, his head bent over his books, as always. Sahil felt a pang of concern. Aniket was brilliant, no doubt about that. But the constant pressure seemed to weigh on him like a heavy burden.

"Aniket's killing himself with all that studying," Sahil muttered, more to himself than to Rohan. "He's like a machine."

Rohan nodded. "Yeah, but look where it's gotten him. He's at the top. Everyone respects him."

"At what cost?" Sahil's voice was soft, filled with quiet sadness. "He never seems to enjoy anything. He's always stressed."

Rohan shrugged. "Maybe that's the price of success."

Sahil didn't answer. He couldn't deny that Aniket was successful, but he wondered if success should come at the expense of happiness.

The bell rang, ending the lunch break. Sahil stuffed the motor into his bag, his mind still buzzing with questions. As they headed back inside, he glanced once more at the library window, the image of Aniket etched in his mind.

The afternoon dragged on, each class a battle for Aniket to stay focused. His head throbbed; his eyes stung from staring at the board for so long. The familiar tightness in his chest grew worse with each passing hour. He couldn't slip now. Not when he had come so far.

As the final bell rang, Aniket packed his bag slowly, his body heavy with exhaustion. He knew he should go home and dive into his homework, but the thought of more studying made him feel sick.

On his way out, he noticed a group of boys gathered under a tree, their voices filled with laughter and excitement. Curious, he wandered over and saw Sahil at the center, working on a small go-kart made from scraps.

"Hey, Aniket!" Rohan called out. "Check this out—Sahil's building a go-kart!"

Aniket approached, amazed. "Did you make this?"

Sahil looked up, grinning. "Yeah, with a little help. It's not much, but it's ours."

Aniket nodded, impressed. "It's amazing. I didn't know you could do this."

Sahil shrugged, his grin modest. "It's fun. Nothing fancy."

Aniket watched as Sahil worked, his hands moving deftly, his expression focused yet relaxed. For the first time, Aniket saw his friend truly in his element, and he realized that this was what made Sahil come alive.

"What about school?" Aniket asked hesitantly. "Aren't you worried about falling behind?"

Sahil paused, looking serious. "I know school's important. But this—this keeps me sane."

Aniket felt a surge of uncertainty. Sahil seemed so free, so unburdened by the constant need to be perfect. Was that the real key to happiness?

"You should try it sometime," Sahil said lightly. "Take a break from the books. Get your hands dirty. It might be good for you."

Aniket chuckled, though unease lingered in his chest. "I wouldn't know where to start."

Sahil smiled, his eyes twinkling. "I'll teach you. It's not that hard."

Aniket hesitated, torn between the pressure of maintaining perfection and the growing desire to break free. "I'll think about it," he said quietly.

Sahil nodded, still smiling. "No rush. Just don't forget to live a little."

Aniket walked away, his mind swirling with conflicting thoughts. He knew Sahil was right. The endless pressure to be perfect was suffocating, but he didn't know how to let go.

As the days passed, Aniket found himself spiralling deeper into exhaustion. The exams loomed closer, and every waking moment was consumed by studying. He stayed up later and later, pushing himself to the brink, terrified of making a mistake. Perfection was no longer a goal; it had become his prison.

Meanwhile, Sahil continued to spend his free time in the backyard, tinkering with machines, dreaming of possibilities. One evening, as he worked on the go-kart, his father approached, his face stern.

"Sahil, you should be studying," his father said sharply. "Exams are coming up."

"I will, Dad. I just needed a break," Sahil replied, trying to keep his frustration in check.

His father's expression hardened. "You're wasting time with these toys. You need to focus on what matters—your future."

Sahil looked down at the motor, his hands still. "This is my future, Dad. Or at least, it's part of it."

His father's voice rose, angry and incredulous. "You think this will get you anywhere in life? You're being irresponsible!"

Sahil clenched his fists, his voice shaking. "At least I'm doing something I love. I can't live my life just ticking boxes and memorizing facts."

His father glared at him before turning and walking away, leaving Sahil alone in the twilight. As the night deepened, Sahil made a quiet vow: he wouldn't give up. He would carve his own path, no matter how difficult.

And so, Aniket and Sahil continued their separate journeys, one chasing perfection, the other fighting for freedom. Both boys were bound by the weight of their choices, neither fully understanding the cost.

For Aniket, the relentless pursuit of perfection came at the expense of joy and peace. For Sahil, the price of freedom was standing alone against the tide of expectation. The road ahead would not be easy, and the decisions they made would shape them in ways they couldn't yet foresee.

Perfection, Sahil realized, was not the shining ideal it was made out to be. It was a heavy burden, one that weighed down the soul, demanding more than anyone could reasonably give. He had watched Aniket, day after day, pushing himself to the limit, sacrificing joy and spontaneity for flawless marks on a page. And for what? To impress teachers, to meet expectations, to tick off accomplishments that felt hollow in the end? Sahil could see the toll it was taking on his friend—the tired eyes, the constant pressure, the lack of laughter. He understood now that perfection was a cage, trapping those who chased it in a cycle of endless striving. It wasn't the path to happiness; it was the path to burnout.

On the other hand, Aniket found himself questioning the rigid structure he had always clung to. Watching Sahil tinker with his machines, lost in his own world of creativity, Aniket began to see freedom in a new light. Sahil didn't have a meticulously mapped-out future, but he seemed content in a way that Aniket wasn't. There was joy in Sahil's work, a sense of discovery and exploration that Aniket had long forgotten. For the first time, Aniket wondered if stepping off the path, even for a moment, might bring him something he desperately needed—space to breathe, room to fail, and the opportunity to find fulfilment beyond perfection. Maybe freedom wasn't reckless; maybe it was necessary. And perhaps, Aniket thought with growing clarity, the risk of letting go of control was a risk worth taking.

CHAPTER SIX

Crossroads of Dreams

The auditorium buzzed with excitement, filled with the hum of voices and the shuffle of feet as students and parents found their seats. The stage, adorned with flowers and banners, stood as a symbol of accomplishment. It was graduation day—the culmination of years of dedication and hard work.

Backstage, Aniket stood with his heart pounding in his chest. He glanced down at his neatly pressed gown, the valedictorian sash draped over his shoulder. This was supposed to be the proudest day of his life, but the familiar tight knot of anxiety twisted in his stomach. He had rehearsed his speech countless times—each word carefully chosen; each sentence polished to perfection. But standing here now, with the weight of his parents' and teachers' expectations pressing down, he couldn't help but feel doubt creeping in.

"Aniket, are you ready?" Miss Rao's voice brought him back to the present. She stood beside him, her eyes warm with pride.

He nodded, forcing a smile. "Yes, ma'am. I'm ready."

She squeezed his shoulder gently. "You'll do great. Just speak from your heart."

Aniket nodded again, but inside, his heart raced like a storm.

Out in the audience, Sahil sat quietly with his parents. The cap and gown he wore felt awkward, unfamiliar, as if they didn't truly belong to him. He had barely scraped through his exams, still relieved to have passed at all. There was no special sash draped over his shoulder, no recognition for his struggles, but he didn't mind. He had made it, and that was enough.

His father's face, however, was a mask of disappointment, while his mother's eyes were clouded with worry. Sahil could sense their unspoken discontent. They had hoped for more. They had expected more. But Sahil couldn't bring himself to feel guilty. He had done his best. That should have been enough.

His mother placed a soft hand on his arm. "Are you okay?"

Sahil nodded. "Yeah, Mom. I'm fine."

"We're proud of you," she whispered, though the sadness in her eyes lingered.

He smiled briefly, though the weight of their expectations still hung heavy over him.

His father shifted in his seat, glancing toward the stage. "This is just the beginning, Sahil. You need to start planning what comes next."

The words hit hard. Sahil knew what his father meant—more expectations, more demands, more pressure.

"I'll figure it out," Sahil said, his voice calm, though uncertainty tugged at him.

The lights dimmed, and the principal's voice boomed through the speakers as he welcomed everyone to the ceremony. Backstage, Aniket's hands tightened into fists. He could hear the applause, the murmurs of approval, but it all felt distant, as if it were happening to someone else.

Then, his name was called.

Aniket stepped forward, the spotlight blinding him for a moment as he made his way to the podium. The auditorium grew silent. Every eye was on him. He glanced at his parents in the front row, their faces glowing with pride. His teachers smiled, encouraging him silently. Then he saw Sahil, sitting further back, his expression unreadable.

Aniket took a deep breath, gripping the edges of the podium. The neatly typed speech lay before him, but suddenly, the words wouldn't come. Panic surged through him, his mind blank.

For a moment, he stood frozen. The silence stretched uncomfortably. He could feel the pressure—expectations from all directions pressing down on him, suffocating him.

He glanced at his parents again, their smiles wavering, concern creeping into their eyes. Then something inside him shifted. He thought about all the late nights, the relentless drive for perfection, and the fear of failure that had haunted him. And then, he thought of Sahil—Sahil, who refused to bend to the same pressures, who embraced his own path, even if it was unconventional.

Aniket inhaled deeply, his mind clearing as he spoke—not from the neatly prepared script, but from the heart.

"When I was asked to give this speech, I thought I had to say all the right things," Aniket began, his voice steady. "I thought I needed to talk about hard work, dedication, and the importance of success. But today, I realize that success means different things to different people. For some, it's about getting the best grades or landing a prestigious job. But for others, success is about finding their own way and their own happiness."

He paused, looking around the room, the words flowing naturally. "I've spent most of my life chasing perfection, trying to meet the expectations of others. And in doing so, I forgot to ask myself what I really wanted. I forgot that success isn't about being the best in the eyes of others; it's about becoming the best version of yourself."

Aniket glanced at Sahil, who met his gaze with an expression that was equal parts surprise and respect.

"So, as we move forward in life," Aniket continued, "I hope we all find the courage to follow our own paths. I hope we have the strength to pursue our dreams, even if they don't fit the neat boxes that society sets out for us. Success isn't about accolades or titles—it's about living authentically."

The silence that followed his words was thick, but it soon gave way to applause that filled the room. Aniket stepped down from the stage, his heart lighter than it had been in years.

His parents rushed to him, eyes brimming with pride. "That was beautiful, Aniket," his mother said, tears glistening in her eyes. "We're so proud of you."

His father nodded; his voice thick with emotion. "You've made us proud, son."

But as Aniket basked in their approval, his eyes scanned the crowd for Sahil, who had quietly slipped out of the auditorium.

Sahil wandered the empty halls of the school, his mind reeling from Aniket's unexpected words. His friend's speech had struck a chord deep within him, resonating with his own doubts, his own struggles.

After the function ended, all the friends gathered one last time, their laughter mixing with the warm evening air as they shared stories, jokes, and memories. It was a bittersweet moment—each of them knew that after today, they would march on different paths, stepping into lives that no longer revolved around shared classrooms and carefree recesses. The air was filled with the weight of unspoken goodbyes, and soon, one by one, they began to disperse, bidding farewell with tight hugs, promises to stay in touch, and a few tears hidden behind brave smiles.

As the crowd thinned and the chatter faded, Aniket and Sahil remained behind, sitting together on the low wall near the school's entrance. The familiar brick under their hands felt oddly comforting, a solid reminder of the place where they had spent years building friendships, facing challenges, and dreaming of futures that now seemed all too real.

For a long moment, they sat in silence, watching the last of their classmates' drift away, their voices growing softer with the distance. The graduation ceremony had been meant to celebrate their accomplishments, but for Aniket and Sahil, it felt like the close of a chapter they weren't entirely ready to end. The excitement of the day had given way to a sense of heaviness, of stepping into an unknown future that stretched out before them with uncertainty.

"Feels strange, doesn't it?" Sahil broke the silence, his voice quiet. "Knowing we won't be walking through those gates as students again."

Aniket nodded, his eyes fixed on the school building. "Yeah. It does. It's like everything we knew is just... ending."

Sahil sighed, running a hand through his hair. "And now, we have to figure out what comes next. You're heading for that prestigious engineering college, like everyone expects. But for me... I don't know, Aniket. I wanted to get into one too, but I'm not sure I fit in that world."

Aniket looked over at Sahil, sensing the doubt in his friend's voice. "You're smart, Sahil. You've got something most people don't—creativity, the ability to think outside the box. That's something no system can measure."

Sahil smiled faintly, but there was sadness in his eyes. "Maybe. But the system doesn't value that. Not when it comes to getting into those top colleges. They want numbers, formulas, facts... and I'm more about ideas, imagination. It's hard when what you're good at doesn't fit into the mould."

Aniket felt a knot tighten in his chest. He had always admired Sahil's ability to think differently, to see the world through a lens of curiosity and creativity. But now, as they stood at the brink of adulthood, he realized that their paths might lead them in opposite directions. He had always known what was expected of him: study hard, get into a top engineering school, make his parents proud. But Sahil's journey was different—less certain, more open-ended.

"We're taking different paths," Aniket said softly, echoing his thoughts. "But that doesn't mean yours is any less important. You'll find your way, Sahil. Even if it's not through the door everyone expects you to walk through."

Sahil looked at him, gratitude and uncertainty flickering in his eyes. "I hope so. I just don't want to lose myself trying to be what everyone else thinks I should be."

Aniket nodded, understanding the weight of Sahil's words. They had spent so many years in a system that defined success in rigid terms, but standing here, on the last day of their school lives, Aniket realized that success was something they would each have to define for themselves.

The sun was beginning to set, casting a warm glow over the school grounds. The moment felt heavy, final. Neither of them spoke for a while, simply sitting side by side, taking in the quiet of the evening and the reality of their impending futures.

"I'll miss this place," Sahil said finally, his voice barely above a whisper. "But more than that, I'll miss us. The way things were."

"Yeah," Aniket agreed, his heart heavy. "But maybe it's time for new things."

They exchanged a glance, one filled with the weight of everything left unsaid. There were no grand promises or long speeches—just the quiet understanding that, whatever happened, they had been a part of each other's lives in a way that would never fade.

As the final rays of sunlight dipped below the horizon, Sahil stood up, dusting off his hands. "Well, I guess this is it, huh?"

Aniket stood as well, his legs feeling heavier than they should. "Yeah. I guess so."

They stood there for a moment longer, before Sahil extended his hand. Aniket took it, and they shook hands, their grip firm but filled with emotion.

"Good luck, Aniket," Sahil said, his voice thick. "You're going to do great things, man."

"You too, Sahil," Aniket replied, his voice quieter. "Whatever you do, you'll make it count."

With one last shared smile, they turned and walked in opposite directions—Aniket heading toward the structured world of engineering, Sahil toward a future still shrouded in uncertainty. Two friends, once so close, now walking different paths—one, the path of a first bencher, clear and precise; the other, the path of a last bencher, uncertain but filled with possibility.

And though they walked away from each other, both knew that the bond they shared would remain, a silent thread connecting them through the years, no matter where life took them.

CHAPTER SEVEN

The Golden Cage

The soft hum of the coffee machine filled the break room, a subtle but constant background noise. Aniket stood in the corner; his gaze fixed on the brown liquid slowly dripping into his cup. The familiar aroma of freshly brewed coffee swirled around him, grounding him in the sterile, impersonal environment of his new office at GenX Solutions—a prestigious tech firm where he had secured a highly coveted position as a junior analyst. Six years had passed since he graduated from engineering school, and after completing an MBA from one of the top institutes in the country, this was supposed to be the reward for all his hard work.

His parents had been elated when the offer letter arrived. His friends looked at him with a mixture of admiration and envy, congratulating him for climbing yet another rung of the corporate ladder. But standing here now, in a neatly pressed suit, surrounded by professionals who exuded confidence, Aniket felt a strange sense of displacement.

The cup warmed his hand, but a knot of anxiety twisted inside his stomach. Taking a sip of the coffee, he let the bitterness slide down his throat, but it did little to settle his nerves. His eyes wandered around the break room, watching as his colleagues moved with practiced ease, their voices a casual hum of light conversation.

"Aniket, right?" A voice interrupted his thoughts. He turned to see a young woman smiling at him, her ID badge displaying her name—Meera Singh, Senior Analyst.

"Yes, that's me. Aniket Mehta," he replied, forcing a polite smile.

"Welcome to GenX," she said, her voice warm and welcoming. "I remember my first day here. It's a lot to take in, isn't it?"

Aniket nodded, his smile tight. "It is. There's so much to learn. I just hope I don't mess up."

Meera laughed lightly, a comforting sound that seemed to ease some of the tension he was carrying. "You'll be fine. Everyone feels overwhelmed at first, but you'll get the hang of it. And if you need any help, just ask."

"Thanks, I appreciate that," he said, a bit of the weight lifting off his shoulders.

Meera gave him an encouraging nod. "We're all in this together. It's a demanding job, but also rewarding. You just have to find the balance."

Balance. Aniket nodded again, though the word felt foreign to him. For so long, life had been a straight line: good grades, engineering, MBA, prestigious job. It was a formula he had followed meticulously. But now, in this corporate maze, it felt like he was a small cog in an enormous machine.

Meera glanced at her watch. "I've got to run to a meeting, but we'll catch up later. Welcome aboard!" she said, her footsteps echoing down the hall as she left.

Aniket sipped his coffee again, the warmth now fading. This was everything he had worked for, everything his parents had dreamed of for him: a stable job, financial security, respect. But instead of the sense of accomplishment he had expected, all he could feel was doubt. Why wasn't this enough? Why did it feel like something was missing?

He shook his head, silently berating himself. This was not the time for self-pity. He had worked too hard to get here, sacrificed too much. He needed to focus, to prove to himself and everyone else that he belonged here.

The rest of the day passed in a blur of introductions, onboarding, and meetings. Aniket found himself submerged in the technical jargon of corporate life, trying to absorb it all while keeping his anxiety at bay. His manager, Mr. Sujoy, was a stern man, his eyes sharp and unforgiving.

He called Aniket to his cabin for the first introduction. Mr. Sujoy sat behind his large, minimalist desk, adjusting his glasses as Aniket took a seat in front of him. The office was sleek and modern, with floor-to-ceiling windows offering a sweeping view of the city skyline. Aniket's palms were slightly damp, a telltale sign of his nerves, but he maintained a composed expression as he faced his manager.

"Aniket, I've looked at your profile," Mr. Sujoy began, his voice calm yet authoritative. "You've got an impressive academic record—engineering from a top college, an MBA from one of the best institutes. Clearly, you've worked hard to get here."

Aniket nodded, feeling a flicker of pride. "Thank you, sir."

"But let me make something clear from the start," Mr. Sujoy continued, leaning forward slightly. "GenX Solutions is not a place where you can rest on your laurels. Yes, you were hired because you showed potential—potential to grow, to contribute, to bring something valuable to the team. But potential alone isn't enough."

Aniket felt his heartbeat quicken slightly as Mr. Sujoy's tone shifted. There was a seriousness to his words that made it clear this wasn't just another onboarding pep talk.

"You see, this company has built its reputation on meeting deadlines, delivering results, and exceeding client expectations," Mr. Sujoy said, his sharp eyes locking onto Aniket's. "It's what sets us apart from our competitors. Clients come to us because they know we deliver. Every single time."

Aniket nodded again, feeling the weight of the expectations grow heavier. He had read about the company's reputation for efficiency and precision, but hearing it directly from his manager made it feel more tangible—and more daunting.

"Now, I'm not here to intimidate you," Mr. Sujoy said, his tone softening slightly. "I understand that this is your first corporate job, and the transition can be challenging. There's a lot to learn, and it can feel overwhelming at times. But know this: we value discipline here, and we expect you to uphold that standard."

Aniket swallowed and cleared his throat. "I understand, sir. I'll do my best to meet the company's expectations."

"I'm sure you will," Mr. Sujoy said, nodding slightly. "But let me be very clear about one thing: deadlines are non-negotiable. If a client expects a project to be delivered by a certain date, it's our job to ensure that happens, no matter what. It doesn't matter if it means working late nights, sacrificing weekends, or missing out on personal time. The brand image of GenX Solutions depends on our reliability."

Aniket shifted in his seat, absorbing the gravity of Mr. Sujoy's words. He had always been diligent, but the stakes felt higher here. It wasn't just about personal achievement anymore; it was about upholding the company's reputation in a fiercely competitive market.

"This is why we offer the kind of compensation packages we do," Mr. Sujoy continued, leaning back in his chair. "We pay you well because we expect a level of commitment and performance that goes beyond just showing up and doing the bare minimum. The corporate environment is demanding, Aniket. It will require sacrifices—sometimes personal, sometimes professional—but that's the price of success here."

Aniket nodded, the enormity of the situation settling in. He had heard stories from friends who had entered the corporate world, stories of long hours and high-pressure environments, but this felt different. It wasn't just about managing tasks—it was about survival.

"I'm not saying this to scare you," Mr. Sujoy added, his voice slightly softer. "But I want you to go into this with your eyes open. We value hard work, but more than that, we value results. If you're struggling, come to me. If you have questions, ask. But know that mistakes are costly. We can't afford them—not when clients are on the line, and not when our reputation is at stake."

Aniket straightened in his seat, meeting Mr. Sujoy's gaze. "I understand, sir. I'll make sure to meet those expectations."

"Good," Mr. Sujoy said, a faint smile appearing on his face for the first time. "I believe you will. Just remember—this isn't just about surviving; it's about thriving. If you can handle the pressure and deliver, you'll go far here. But if you falter... well, let's just say the competition is always ready to take your place."

Aniket nodded, feeling the weight of those words settle on him. He had faced pressure before—in exams, in interviews, in his academic career—but this felt different. This was real. The stakes were higher, and the consequences more immediate.

"You're smart, Aniket," Mr. Sujoy said, standing up and extending his hand. "But intelligence is just the starting point. It's how you use it under pressure that matters."

Aniket shook his hand, the firm grip a reminder of the challenges ahead. "Thank you, sir. I won't let you down."

"I'm counting on it," Mr. Sujoy replied, releasing his hand. "Now get to work. There's a lot to do."

Aniket nodded. He knew this pressure well—it had driven him through school and college, had fuelled his every decision. But the stakes felt higher now, the consequences more real.

As the sun dipped behind the city skyline and the office began to empty, Aniket made his way to the train station. The crowded platform was a stark contrast to the orderly world of the office. As he waited for the train, he noticed the weary faces around him, people locked in their own routines, moving through life with the same monotony. Was this it? Was this the life he had worked so hard for?

The train screeched to a halt, and Aniket stepped inside, finding a seat by the window. The city lights flickered past, but all he could think about was Sahil.

Sahil had been his opposite in many ways. After failing to secure a spot in a prestigious engineering college, Sahil had gone to a local institution, his future shaped more by his imagination than by the linear path society laid out. While Aniket had followed the straight and narrow—engineering, MBA, corporate career—Sahil had meandered. He tinkered, explored, and experimented, never quite fitting into any box.

Aniket's phone buzzed, pulling him from his thoughts. It was a message from Sahil.

"How's the first day at the big job?" the text read, cheerful as always.

Aniket typed a quick reply. "It's... intense. There's a lot to take in."

Sahil responded almost immediately. "That's how it is at the start. Don't worry, you'll figure it out. You always do."

Aniket smiled despite himself. Sahil had always been the optimist, even when the odds were against him.

"What about you? How's the workshop coming along?" Aniket asked.

"Slow but steady," came Sahil's reply. "I'm thinking of expanding, but we'll see. Still figuring things out. Honestly, I envy you. You've got it all planned."

Aniket stared at the words. Was his life really that enviable? On paper, maybe. But in reality, it felt like he was trapped in a cycle, his dreams and desires smothered under layers of obligation and routine.

He typed slowly, choosing his words carefully. "Yeah, but it's hard. I feel like I'm stuck in a loop."

Sahil's response was immediate. "That's the thing about loops. Sometimes you have to break out of them to see the whole picture. Maybe you need to ask yourself what *you* want, not what everyone else wants for you."

Aniket read the message again, feeling the weight of the words. Sahil had always lived on his own terms, unbound by expectations. And while that path came with its own set of challenges, it was a freedom Aniket had never allowed himself to explore.

The train slowed as it approached his stop. Aniket stood up, gripping his phone tightly. "Maybe you're right. Let's catch up this weekend," he typed before stepping off the train.

The next few days passed in a blur of long hours and even longer nights. Aniket threw himself into his work, determined to live up to the expectations that had been set for him. His dedication did not go unnoticed—Mr. Sujoy praised his work, and his colleagues quickly came to respect his meticulous attention to detail. But the praise felt hollow, like the echo of a sound that had lost its meaning.

Saturday arrived, and for the first time in months, Aniket felt a sense of relief as he made his way to the cafe where Sahil had suggested they meet. When he arrived, Sahil was already there, his face lit with the easy smile that Aniket had always envied.

"So, how's life in the corporate world?" Sahil asked, leaning back in his chair with a relaxed ease.

"It's... a lot," Aniket admitted. "It's what I've always worked for, but it feels... empty."

Sahil nodded, his expression thoughtful. "That's because it's what you worked for, not necessarily what you wanted."

Aniket looked down at his coffee, the truth of Sahil's words hitting harder than he expected.

"I guess I've been on autopilot for so long, I didn't realize it," Aniket said.

Sahil smiled. "It's never too late to hit the brakes, man. You've got a lot going for you, but you've also got to figure out what makes you happy."

Aniket nodded, feeling something loosen inside him, like a weight had been lifted. For the first time in years, he allowed himself to think about what *he* wanted—not his parents, not society, but him.

As they walked through the city, the sun setting behind the skyscrapers, Aniket realized that success didn't have to mean living in a gilded cage. He could break free. He could build something new, something his own.

And as he watched the city lights flicker on, he knew that the first step was simply allowing himself to want more.

CHAPTER EIGHT

The Weight of Expectations

The soft hum of the coffee machine was almost drowned out by the relentless ticking of the clock on the wall, a constant reminder of the passing time. Aniket sat at his desk, the glow of his computer screen illuminating the tired lines of his face. He wasn't the only one still at the office—it was past midnight, but the office was far from quiet. His colleagues, like him, were hunched over their desks, fingers flying across keyboards, racing to meet deadlines that seemed to stretch on forever.

It had been three months since Aniket had started his job at GenX Solutions, and already the excitement of joining a prestigious tech firm had worn off. The pride his parents had felt when he landed the role, the admiration of his friends, all of it now felt like a distant memory. Instead, a crushing sense of disillusionment had settled in its place.

The glow of success had faded, revealing the harsh reality beneath. The long hours, the ceaseless demands, the unrelenting pressure to perform—it was all starting to weigh him down. He had followed the path laid out for him meticulously: good grades, engineering, an MBA from a top institute, and finally, the job at GenX. But now, he wasn't sure if this was the path he wanted to be on anymore.

"Still burning the midnight oil?" a familiar voice pulled him from his thoughts. It was Reha, a fellow junior analyst who had joined the company a few months before him. She looked as tired as he felt, dark circles under her eyes, her face drawn with exhaustion.

Aniket forced a smile. "Yeah, just trying to finish up this report for Sujoy. You know how it is."

Reha sighed and leaned against his cubicle. "Tell me about it. I've been working on the Johnson project non-stop for the past two weeks. Sujoy's been on my case about it too. I'm starting to think he never sleeps."

Aniket let out a dry laugh, though there was little humour in it. "Maybe he's a machine. That would explain a lot."

Reha gave a half-smile, but there was no hiding the weariness in her voice. "It feels like that's what they want from us, doesn't it? To be machines. No emotions, no personal life—just work."

Aniket nodded, staring at the spreadsheet in front of him. "I didn't think it would be like this. I thought... I don't know, I thought it would feel more fulfilling."

Reha's expression softened, and she nodded in understanding. "I know what you mean. I used to be excited about coming to work. Now it's just... routine. But what choice do we have? This is the job we signed up for."

Aniket didn't answer. He knew she was right. This was the life he had chosen, the one he had worked so hard to achieve. The big salary, the prestigious title—it was everything he had dreamed of. But the dream was turning into a nightmare, one where he couldn't escape the suffocating weight of his responsibilities.

"It's just that," Aniket hesitated, choosing his words carefully, "it feels like we're giving everything to this job and getting nothing back. I mean, sure, the pay is great, but at what cost? I haven't had a weekend to myself in months. My friends barely see me anymore. I'm constantly exhausted. Is this really what we worked so hard for?"

Reha sighed, her shoulders slumping slightly. "That's the thing, isn't it? The company pays us well, and they expect us to give everything in return. Time, energy, health—it all belongs to them now."

She was right. Aniket knew it. His job had consumed every aspect of his life. His weekends, once filled with relaxation or hobbies, had been reduced to endless hours spent catching up on work. Even when he wasn't at the office, he was mentally tethered to it, his thoughts constantly revolving around deadlines, presentations, and client meetings.

"I guess that's the price we pay," Aniket said quietly, more to himself than to Rhea.

Just then, his phone buzzed on the desk. It was a message from Sujoy, his supervisor: *"I need that report on my desk by 7 AM. No excuses."*

Aniket felt a familiar sinking feeling in his chest. It was already past midnight, and the thought of staying even later was unbearable. But he had no choice. There were never any choices in this place.

Reha glanced at his phone and shook her head. "Sujoy again? He really knows how to push people to the edge."

Aniket gave a bitter laugh. "Yeah, well, he's good at what he does, I'll give him that."

Reha's eyes darkened. "He's good at making people burn out, that's what he is. You know, the other day I heard him talking to one of the senior managers. They were saying something about how they expect us to make sacrifices—that it's part of the job if we want to survive here."

"Sacrifices?" Aniket asked, raising an eyebrow.

"Yeah," Reha nodded. "They were talking about how the company's reputation depends on meeting deadlines and delivering results, no matter what it takes. If we have to give up our personal lives, our health, our sanity... well, that's just part of the deal. They pay us big salaries, and in return, we're expected to give up everything else."

Aniket stared at her, feeling a cold chill settle in his stomach. He had always known the job was demanding, but hearing it put so bluntly made it more real. The company didn't care about him, about Reha, or about any of the other employees. They were just tools, cogs in the machine that drove the company's success. And if one cog broke down, it would be replaced without a second thought.

"It's like we're trapped," Aniket said, his voice barely above a whisper.

Reha looked at him for a long moment, then nodded slowly. "That's exactly it. We're trapped. And the worst part is, we did this to ourselves. We worked so hard to get here, thinking it was the dream. But now we're stuck in it, and there's no way out."

Aniket stared at the screen in front of him, the endless rows of data blurring together as exhaustion and frustration clouded his mind. He had followed the path laid out for him his entire life—good grades, engineering, MBA, a prestigious job—and now, here he was, a prisoner of his own success.

He thought about quitting, about walking into Sujoy's office and handing in his resignation. But the thought filled him with dread. What would his parents say? They had been so proud when he got the job at GenX Solutions. What about the expectations of his friends, who looked up to him as a success story? And then there was the financial security. Leaving the job meant giving up the comfortable salary, the benefits, the safety net he had worked so hard to create.

Could he really walk away from all of that? Could he abandon the life he had built, even if it wasn't making him happy?

Aniket glanced at Reha, who was watching him with a knowing look.

"You're thinking about quitting, aren't you?" she asked softly.

Aniket didn't answer right away. He wasn't sure if he was ready to admit it, even to himself. Finally, he nodded. "Yeah. Sometimes I think about it. But... I don't know if I can."

Reha gave him a sad smile. "I get it. It's not easy. We've built our lives around this idea of success, and walking away from it feels like failure. But you have to ask yourself, is this really the life you want?"

Aniket didn't respond. The truth was, he didn't know what he wanted anymore. All he knew was that he was tired—tired of the endless grind, the unrelenting pressure, the hollow feeling that came with each completed task. But leaving wasn't an option, not yet. He wasn't ready to face the disappointment of his parents, the judgment of his peers. And so, he stayed.

The days turned into weeks, and Aniket found himself sinking deeper into the routine. The late nights became more frequent, the deadlines more demanding. Sujoy's emails never stopped, each one a reminder that failure was not an option. His body grew heavier with each passing day, weighed down by exhaustion and a growing sense of hopelessness.

One evening, as he sat alone in the office long after everyone else had left, Aniket received a call from Sahil. It had been weeks since they last spoke, and the sound of his friend's voice was a welcome break from the monotony.

"How's the corporate grind treating you, man?" Sahil asked, his tone light, but with an undercurrent of concern.

Aniket leaned back in his chair, closing his eyes. "It's... rough. I'm barely keeping my head above water."

Sahil was silent for a moment before speaking again. "You don't sound like yourself, Aniket. What's going on?"

Aniket hesitated, unsure of how to explain the slow erosion of his spirit. "I don't know. It's like... I thought this job would be the pinnacle, you know? The thing I've worked for my entire life. But now that I'm here, I don't feel... anything."

Sahil's voice softened. "That's because you're chasing someone else's dream, man. You've always been the one to follow the rules, to do what's expected of you. But maybe it's time to start thinking about what *you* want."

Aniket sighed. "I wish it were that simple. There's so much riding on this—my parents, my friends, the money. I can't just walk away."

"You don't have to walk away right now," Sahil said gently. "But you need to figure out what's making you unhappy. Otherwise, this job is going to eat you alive."

Aniket nodded, though Sahil couldn't see him. He knew his friend was right. The job was already taking its toll on him—physically, emotionally, mentally. But leaving wasn't an option. Not yet.

As Aniket hung up the phone and returned to his work, he realized that the golden cage he had built for himself was tighter than ever. He wasn't ready to leave it, not now. But the thought of staying in it, of slowly losing himself to the grind, was unbearable.

For now, all he could do was accept his fate, hoping that someday, he would find the courage to break free.

CHAPTER NINE

The Rocky Road

The morning sunlight filtered through the dusty windows of Mr. Sharma's small garage, casting long, slanting rays across the scattered tools and spare parts that littered the workbenches. The hum of machines and the metallic clinking of tools filled the air, accompanied by the occasional burst of conversation between the mechanics. Amid the clutter and chaos, Sahil stood hunched over an old motorbike, his hands greasy and worn, tightening bolts and adjusting parts with practiced ease.

It had been two weeks since Sahil had started working at the local auto repair shop, a decision born out of necessity rather than choice. His dreams of opening his own workshop and building something from scratch were still there, but they felt distant now, buried beneath the heavy weight of financial strain and survival. Mr. Sharma's garage was far from the future Sahil had envisioned for himself, but for now, it was a lifeline.

The pay was modest, just enough to cover his rent and basic expenses. It wasn't ideal, but it kept him going. He wasn't giving up on his dreams—he was just finding a way to keep them alive.

"Hey, Sahil!" Mr. Sharma's voice rang out from across the garage, booming over the sound of engines and tools. He was a stout man, his gruff voice softened by the lines of kindness etched into his face. "How's that bike coming along? The customer's been asking for it since yesterday."

Sahil glanced up, wiping sweat from his brow with the back of his hand. His face, streaked with grease and exhaustion, betrayed the long hours he had been putting in. "Almost done, sir. Just fixing the alignment issue. Should be good in about ten minutes."

Mr. Sharma nodded, his expression softening. "Good job, lad. You've got a knack for this. Not many can figure out these old machines the way you do."

Sahil managed a small smile. Compliments like that from Mr. Sharma were rare, and he appreciated the acknowledgment. "Thanks, sir. I've always enjoyed working with my hands. It just... makes sense to me."

"Keep it up, Sahil," Mr. Sharma said, clapping him on the shoulder before heading back to his own work. "You've got potential. Just remember, we all have to start somewhere."

Sahil watched Mr. Sharma walk away, the weight of his words hanging in the air. He knew Mr. Sharma meant well, and he was grateful for the opportunity. But as much as he respected the old man, this wasn't where he wanted to be forever. The garage, with its oil-soaked floors and rusty tools, wasn't the future Sahil had envisioned for himself. His ambitions reached far beyond fixing motorbikes for meagre wages. He wanted to build something, to innovate, to create something that was truly his own.

But for now, survival came first.

As the engine of the old motorbike roared to life under his hands, Sahil felt a flicker of pride. It was a small victory, hearing the steady purr of the engine after hours of meticulous work. But even as the satisfaction settled over him, a deeper, nagging frustration lingered. His dreams of owning his own workshop, of designing and building new machines, felt like they were slipping further away with each passing day.

He stepped out of the garage, squinting against the bright sunlight as he made his way to the small tea stall across the street. The owner, Raju, greeted him with a toothy grin.

"Sahil! Hard at work again, I see," Raju said, his voice filled with warmth and familiarity. "The usual?"

Sahil nodded, his thoughts still on the motorbike and the long hours ahead. "Yeah, Raju bhai. And throw in an extra samosa today. I'm starving."

Raju chuckled as he poured a steaming cup of tea. "You young people, always in such a rush. Take it easy once in a while, huh?"

Sahil smiled faintly, accepting the cup and the plate of samosas. The warmth of the tea spread through him, easing the tension in his muscles. He leaned against the counter, staring out at the busy street beyond, watching the world pass him by.

People hurried along the sidewalks; their faces etched with the same lines of exhaustion that Sahil felt creeping into his own life. It was a strange feeling—being part of the city's hustle and bustle, yet feeling disconnected from it all. He was just one more person struggling to make it through the day, lost in the noise and chaos of survival.

He thought of Aniket, his friend's face flashing in his mind. Aniket, who had secured a high-paying job at a prestigious firm, who seemed to be on the fast track to success. Sahil felt a familiar pang of envy, but it was quickly followed by pride. Aniket had worked hard for his success. He deserved it. But Sahil couldn't help but wonder where he fit into the grand scheme of things. He had always been the one who refused to follow the well-trodden path, the one who wanted more freedom, more creativity.

"Sahil!" Raju's voice snapped him out of his thoughts. The old man was watching him with a knowing smile. "Lost in thought again, I see?"

Sahil shrugged, a sheepish grin tugging at his lips. "Just thinking about the future, Raju bhai. Trying to figure out where I'm headed."

Raju nodded wisely, his eyes twinkling. "You're young, Sahil. You've got time. Don't rush things. Just keep working hard, and you'll find your way. Rome wasn't built in a day, you know."

Sahil chuckled, taking a bite of his samosa. "Yeah, I know. But sometimes it feels like I'm stuck in the same place, no matter how hard I try."

Raju leaned forward, his voice gentle. "Life is like that sometimes, beta. One step forward, two steps back. But as long as you're moving, you're on the right path."

Sahil nodded, Raju's words lifting some of the weight off his chest. He finished his tea, thanked the old man, and headed back to the garage. The rest of the day passed in a blur of work—fixing engines, replacing parts, talking to customers. His hands moved with the practiced ease of someone who knew the ins and outs of his craft. But despite the satisfaction of a job well done, there was always that lingering feeling that this wasn't enough. That he was meant for more.

By the time the sun began to set, casting the city in a warm orange glow, Sahil was ready to collapse. His body ached from the long hours, his mind buzzing with thoughts of the future, of the plans he had yet to bring to life. As he walked back to his small rented room, the sky darkening above him, the weight of the day seemed to settle heavily on his shoulders.

His room was as modest as his pay check—just enough space for a bed, a small desk, and a chair. But it was his sanctuary. The walls were lined with sketches and blueprints, ideas that had been swirling in his mind for months. Machines he wanted to build, innovations he dreamed of bringing to life. But with each passing day, those dreams felt further out of reach, buried beneath the reality of his situation.

As he lay on his bed, staring up at the cracked ceiling, Sahil's phone buzzed on the bedside table. It was a message from Aniket.

"Hey, Sahil! How's it going?"

Sahil smiled, the sound of Aniket's voice playing in his mind as he typed a reply. "Same old, same old. Working at the garage, trying to keep my head above water. What about you? Climbing that corporate ladder?"

Aniket's response came quickly. "Yeah, something like that. It's been a grind, but I'm managing. Just wanted to check in on you."

Sahil sighed, his tone turning serious as he replied. "It's tough, Aniket. I'm barely scraping by. But I can't give up, you know? I've got to keep pushing."

There was a pause before Aniket replied, his message filled with concern. "You'll make it, Sahil. I know you will. You've always been the one to find a way."

Sahil felt a warmth spread through him at his friend's words. "Thanks, Aniket. That means a lot. But sometimes it feels like I'm just treading water."

"You're not alone in that," Aniket replied. "We all feel like that sometimes. But you've got something special, Sahil. Don't lose sight of that."

Sahil stared at the screen, his heart swelling with gratitude. He and Aniket had always been on different paths, but their bond had never wavered. And even now, as they struggled in their own ways, they were still there for each other.

After they finished talking, Sahil lay in the quiet of his room, his mind racing. He knew he couldn't give up. He had come too far, fought too hard to let go now. Yes, the road was rocky, and yes, the weight of financial strain and daily struggles threatened to pull him under. But he had something worth fighting for—his dreams, his vision, his future.

The next day, Sahil returned to the garage with renewed energy. He threw himself into his work, fixing bikes and talking to customers, learning everything he could from Mr. Sharma. But even as he toiled away in the small garage, his mind was constantly buzzing with ideas. He spent his lunch breaks sketching designs, writing down plans for new machines, dreaming of the day when he could turn those dreams into reality.

One afternoon, a young man walked into the garage, his face etched with worry. He explained that his bike had broken down and that without it, he couldn't work. Sahil could see the desperation in his eyes, and without hesitation, he offered to fix the bike, even though the man couldn't afford to pay him right away. It wasn't about the money—it was about doing the right thing.

As the man rode off on his repaired bike, gratitude shining in his eyes, Sahil felt a sense of satisfaction he hadn't felt in a long time. It was a reminder of why he had chosen this path in the first place. He wanted to help people, to create something that mattered. And no matter how hard things got, he wasn't going to lose sight of that.

As the days turned into weeks, Sahil continued to work at the garage, saving every penny he could. He knew it wouldn't be easy, but he also knew that failure was a part of success. He wasn't afraid to take risks, to keep pushing forward, even if the road was tough.

Because sometimes, the rocky road was the only one worth taking.

CHAPTER TEN

The Web of Security

The fluorescent lights buzzed faintly overhead, casting a sterile glow across the endless rows of cubicles. Aniket sat at his desk, hunched over the glowing screen. Numbers and data filled the spreadsheet before him, but they had begun to blur together after hours of staring at them. His temples throbbed, a dull ache radiating from the base of his skull as the fatigue from working since early morning took its toll.

The clock on his desktop showed it was nearing midnight, yet the emails kept coming, each one marked *urgent*, demanding his attention. His fingers hovered over the keyboard, poised to type, but he hesitated. The pressure was relentless—reports needed analysing, presentations required completion, deadlines loomed like dark clouds on the horizon. He was barely keeping afloat, trying to tread water in a sea of tasks that seemed impossible to conquer.

A gentle knock on the partition broke his concentration. Aniket blinked and looked up to find Meera standing at the entrance to his cubicle, two steaming cups of coffee in her hands. She offered him a tired smile, concern evident in her eyes.

"I thought you could use this," she said, placing one of the cups on his desk.

"Thanks," Aniket mumbled, his voice raw from disuse. He took a sip of the coffee, the bitterness momentarily jolting him awake, though it did little to soothe the growing exhaustion that threatened to overwhelm him.

Meera leaned against the wall of his cubicle, her eyes studying him with quiet concern. "You've been here since dawn, Aniket. You need to take a break."

He let out a dry chuckle, though it lacked any real humour. "I can't. Too much to do. I still have to finish the financial projections for tomorrow's board meeting."

She sighed, her shoulders slumping. "I know, but you're going to burn out if you keep going like this. You're not a machine, Aniket."

He looked at her, a bitter smile curling his lips. "Sometimes I think that's exactly what they want us to be—efficient, emotionless, always working."

Meera didn't respond immediately, her silence heavy with understanding. She had been with the company long enough to know the cycle, to see how the corporate machine ground down even the brightest employees, wearing them out under the constant pressure to perform.

"Have you talked to Mr. Sujoy about getting some help?" she asked after a moment, her voice soft but persistent. "Maybe he could delegate part of your workload."

Aniket snorted, shaking his head. "Mr. Sujoy? He's the one who gave me this mountain of work in the first place. He said it was an 'opportunity'—a chance to prove myself."

Meera frowned, a deep crease forming between her brows. "That doesn't sound like an opportunity. That sounds like exploitation."

Aniket shrugged, the weight of the spreadsheet in front of him pressing down even harder. "It's just how it works. You either play the game, or you get left behind."

Her expression turned sombre. "It's a dangerous game, Aniket. You can lose yourself in it."

Her words lingered in the air, unsettling him in a way he hadn't expected. For a moment, he felt the edges of fear creeping in, like he was teetering on the brink of something darker than mere exhaustion. But he pushed the feeling down, burying it beneath the overwhelming list of tasks still ahead of him.

"I'll be fine," he said, though his tone lacked conviction. "I just need to get through this week."

Meera sighed again but didn't push further. She knew better than anyone how stubborn Aniket could be, how determined he was to prove himself—even at the cost of his own well-being. "Just don't forget to eat," she said gently, her voice tinged with concern. "And if you need anything, I'm here."

Aniket nodded, managing a small, grateful smile. "Thanks, Meera. I appreciate it."

With one last lingering look, she left, her footsteps fading into the hum of the nearly empty office. Aniket watched her go, the sense of loneliness growing heavier. The office was quiet now, the other employees having left hours ago. Yet here he was, still chained to his desk, still working.

He turned back to his computer and forced himself to focus. He had chosen this path. He had worked tirelessly to get to this point. He had believed that success would bring happiness, that achieving his goals would fill the void inside him. But now, as he stared at the endless rows of numbers, he felt only a hollow ache.

Hours passed in a fog of emails, spreadsheets, and presentations. Aniket moved mechanically; his mind dull with fatigue. The clock ticked past seven in the morning, and there was still so much left to do.

His phone buzzed on the desk, pulling him from the haze of work. It was Sahil.

He hadn't spoken to his friend in weeks, their lives diverging so drastically since Aniket had started his corporate climb. Hesitating for a moment, he answered the call, his voice hoarse with exhaustion.

"Hey, Sahil."

"Aniket! Still at work?" Sahil's voice was full of life, a stark contrast to the numbness Aniket felt creeping into his own.

Aniket glanced around the empty office. "Yeah, just finishing up."

"Finishing up? It means you have worked whole night! What are you doing, man? You need to get some sleep!"

Aniket chuckled bitterly. "There's no time for sleep, Sahil. Too many deadlines."

"Deadlines," Sahil repeated, the word heavy with disdain. "You've got to stop pushing yourself like this. You'll drive yourself into the ground."

"I'll be fine," Aniket said, the words automatic. They felt hollow, a mantra he repeated to keep the truth at bay.

Sahil was silent for a moment, then his voice came softer, almost hesitant. "Are you happy, Aniket?"

The question hit him like a punch, leaving him momentarily breathless. *Happy?* He hadn't even thought about happiness in so long. He had been so focused on proving himself, on meeting expectations, that he had forgotten to ask himself if any of it made him happy.

"I'm... doing what I need to do," he said finally, his voice empty.

"That's not what I asked."

Aniket swallowed; his throat tight. "I don't know, Sahil. I don't know."

The silence that followed was heavy, filled with the unspoken truths Aniket had been avoiding for too long. He had always been the one with the plan, the one who had everything figured out. But now, it felt like the plan had led him somewhere he didn't want to be.

"You don't have to have all the answers right now," Sahil said gently. "Just don't lose yourself in the process, okay?"

"I'll try," Aniket whispered, though he wasn't sure he believed it. Then he hesitantly said, "Sahil, I have to finish the work before nine, so I'll talk to you in the evening when I'm free."

He stared at the glowing screen, the cold data staring back at him. He had thought that success would bring freedom, but now he saw that it had only trapped him further, weaving him into a web of security that felt more like a prison with every passing day.

He thought about Mr. Sujoy and the way he pushed him to take on more and more responsibility, calling it "opportunity." But now, he saw it for what it really was—manipulation. He had been caught in the web of corporate politics; his ambition twisted into something exploitable.

Suddenly, he couldn't sit still. He stood up, the chair rolling back with a loud clatter, and grabbed his jacket. The cool morning air hit him like a slap as he stepped outside, taking deep breaths to calm the storm of emotions swirling inside him. He walked aimlessly through the city streets, his mind racing with thoughts of the life he had built for himself, the choices he had made.

He found himself at a small park near the office, the benches empty, the trees casting long shadows in the dim sun light. He sat down, resting his head in his hands, the weight of his decisions pressing down on him. He thought about his parents, their pride when he had told them about his job. He thought about Sahil, who had chosen freedom over security, who had refused to be bound by the expectations that had trapped him.

For the first time, he let himself wonder if he could do the same.

As the first light of dawn began to streak the cloudy sky, Aniket stood up, his heart heavy but resolute. He didn't have all the answers, and he didn't know what the future held. But he knew one thing: he couldn't keep living like this.

He walked back to the office, the city slowly waking around him. The familiar chaos of work awaited him, but there was a small flicker of hope inside him now. He had to find a way to reclaim his life, to break free from the web that had ensnared him.

And for the first time in months, that small spark of hope felt like it was all he needed.

CHAPTER ELEVEN

First Step of Courage

The warm hues of the setting sun filtered through the windows of Sahil's small rented room, casting long shadows over his cluttered workbench. The air was thick with the smell of solder and burnt plastic, a familiar scent in the space filled with half-finished projects and scattered tools. Sahil sat hunched over his work, his hands steady as he soldered a wire to the circuit board in front of him. His face was streaked with dirt and sweat, but his eyes were sharp with focus, his mind racing with possibilities.

For weeks now, Sahil had been working on this project. What had begun as a simple idea had slowly grown into something much more—a prototype for a portable battery charger made from recycled electronic components. It wasn't flashy or groundbreaking by the standards of the tech world, but for Sahil, it represented hope. A chance to create something meaningful from scratch, using only his hands, ingenuity, and scraps of discarded technology.

He leaned back, wiping the sweat from his brow, and examined the device. It was rough, far from perfect, but it was his—a product of endless hours of work, trial and error. More than anything, it was a symbol of his determination to carve out a path for himself. Despite all the uncertainties, despite the challenges, he knew this was a start.

His phone buzzed on the cluttered table, and he saw Aniket's name flash on the screen. A smile tugged at his lips.

"Hey, man," Aniket's voice came through, tired but familiar. "How's the mad scientist act going?"

Sahil chuckled, feeling a surge of warmth at the sound of his friend's voice. "It's going... well, it's something. Almost done with the prototype. Just a few more tweaks."

"That's awesome, Sahil! I knew you'd make it happen. When can I see it?"

Sahil paused, his eyes flicking back to the unfinished device on the table. "Soon, I hope. Just need to make sure it doesn't go up in smoke when I test it."

"Well, I'm sure it'll be great," Aniket said with a confidence that made Sahil's heart lift. "You've worked so hard on this, and I'm proud of you, man."

Sahil felt a lump in his throat, gratitude swelling in his chest. "Thanks, Aniket. It means a lot. But there's still so much to do. This is just the first step."

"First step, but the hardest one," Aniket's voice was filled with encouragement. "Just keep pushing, Sahil. You've got this."

Sahil nodded, his resolve hardening. "I will. Thanks again, Aniket. I really appreciate it. But enough about me, how's work?"

There was a brief silence before Aniket responded, his tone softer, subdued. "It's... fine. Just really busy. But let's focus on your success for now. This is your moment."

Sahil sensed the weariness behind Aniket's words but decided not to press. They both had their struggles, and tonight wasn't the time to delve into them. "Alright, I'll keep you updated. Thanks, Aniket. For everything."

"Anytime, Sahil," Aniket said warmly. "Take care."

As the call ended, Sahil set his phone down, staring at the prototype on the table. His room was quiet now, save for the soft ticking of the clock, and the air felt heavy with anticipation. The excitement he had felt earlier was now mingling with fear. He had taken the first step, but the road ahead remained uncertain. The failure of the prototype loomed large in his mind as he connected the wires, watching the small LED blink to life. For a moment, hope surged through him. But then, with a small pop, the light flickered out, and a thin wisp of smoke curled from the device.

Sahil's heart sank. He stared at the failed prototype, feeling the weight of disappointment press down on him. He had come so close, only for it to slip away in an instant. All those hours, all that effort—it felt like it was for nothing.

He picked up the device, turning it over in his hands as frustration bubbled up inside him. His fingers trembled slightly from exhaustion and anger. Why couldn't it just work? He had put everything he had into this—his time, his energy, his dreams. But once again, he found himself facing failure.

It wasn't the first time. Failure had been a constant companion in this journey. Yet, this time, it felt heavier, more personal, as if the universe was telling him he wasn't cut out for this. He wanted to scream, to throw the device across the room and be done with it. But instead, he forced himself to take a deep breath, placing the prototype gently back on the table.

Sahil rubbed his eyes, the exhaustion catching up with him. He had been working without rest for days, barely sleeping, his mind consumed by the project. But giving up now, even for a moment, felt like defeat. He couldn't afford to stop, not when he was this close.

For a few moments, he sat there in silence, staring at the scattered tools and half-finished projects that surrounded him. The cluttered room felt like a reflection of his mind—chaotic, full of potential, but also full of uncertainty. His hands still shook as he reached for the device, determined to figure out what had gone wrong.

He examined the circuit board again, thinking through every step he had taken, searching for the flaw. His thoughts raced, replaying every choice, every component he had used. Slowly, as the minutes ticked by, his frustration began to give way to focus. It wasn't over. Not yet.

He stood up, stretching his stiff muscles, and glanced out the window at the quiet city streets. It was late, the world outside still and calm, but his mind buzzed with renewed energy. He would try again. He had no choice.

Failure wasn't an end. It was part of the process. He had to remind himself of that. He thought of Aniket's words—the first step is the hardest. It was true. And he had taken that step, even if it had stumbled along the way.

For the next few hours, Sahil worked tirelessly. His movements were slower now, more deliberate. He made adjustments, rechecked his connections, tested the circuits over and over. His fingers were calloused, his body heavy with fatigue, but he kept going.

And then, as the first light of dawn crept through the window, Sahil connected the battery once more. The LED blinked to life, holding steady this time. The soft hum of the device filled the room, and Sahil's breath caught in his throat.

It worked.

He slumped into his chair, relief washing over him like a wave. It wasn't perfect, not yet. But it was a start. He had done it.

A small smile tugged at his lips as he looked at the fragile device on the table. After all the failures, all the doubts, he had taken another step forward. The road ahead was still long, full of unknowns, but for the first time in what felt like months, Sahil felt hope.

He thought of Aniket, of his friend's unwavering support, and of the countless people who had doubted him. And, most of all, he thought of himself—the boy who had been told he didn't belong, who had always felt out of place. The boy who had dared to dream, even when those dreams seemed impossible.

Sahil knew there would be more failures ahead, more obstacles to overcome. But for now, he allowed himself to rest. He allowed himself to feel proud.

Because sometimes, the hardest part isn't building the prototype or creating something new. It's finding the courage to take the first step.

As the sun rose over the city, Sahil closed his eyes, a smile playing at his lips. The promise of a new day stretched out before him, full of possibilities.

CHAPTER TWELVE

The Art of Survival

The office buzzed with the low hum of conversation and the rhythmic clicking of keyboards. Aniket sat in the glass-walled conference room, fingers tapping lightly on the polished table, his mind drifting as Mr. Sujoy explained the new restructuring plan. Corporate jargon filled the air, an all-too-familiar deluge of phrases designed to sound important but devoid of real meaning.

His gaze wandered across the room, taking in the faces of his colleagues. Some appeared engaged, nodding along as if every word was critical to their survival. Others wore the same weary expression that had taken root in his chest—a mixture of fatigue and resignation, the burden of navigating corporate politics weighing heavily on them.

"Aniket, what do you think about the proposed changes to the project timelines?" Mr. Sujoy's voice sliced through his reverie like a sharp blade, pulling him abruptly back to the moment.

Aniket straightened in his chair, his thoughts racing to recall the details of the presentation. He had drifted, lost in his own disillusionment, but now the spotlight was on him. He couldn't afford to falter.

"I believe it's a logical adjustment, sir," he replied, his tone calm and measured. "The revised timeline gives us the flexibility to address the client's concerns and ensure all key deliverables are met. However, we might need to reallocate resources to avoid bottlenecks in the development phase."

Mr. Sujoy gave a nod of approval, though his sharp eyes remained calculating. "Good point. I'll look into reallocating some resources from the marketing team."

Aniket returned the nod, keeping his face impassive. Inside, though, he felt an unsettling sense of detachment. This was his life now—playing the corporate game, manoeuvring through endless meetings, and offering well-crafted responses designed to keep him in the running. He was just another cog in a machine, his individuality buried under layers of corporate expectations.

The meeting dragged on, and Aniket forced himself to participate, his words carefully chosen, his contributions always calculated to be just enough—but not too much. It was a dance he had mastered, an exhausting performance where ambition and submission intertwined in a delicate balance.

When the meeting finally ended, he gathered his materials with slow deliberation and made his way back to his cubicle. He sank into his chair, closing his eyes for a moment as the weight of the day settled over him. It had once been enough to work hard, to stay focused, to believe that success would follow. But now, he understood the truth—survival in this world was about far more than just hard work. It was about alliances, favours, and navigating the invisible web of power that dictated everything.

His gaze fell on the framed photograph on his desk—a picture of him and Sahil from their school days. Their younger faces beamed with optimism; eyes full of dreams. Aniket stared at the photo, the ache in his chest tightening. He had wanted to make a difference, to create something meaningful. Now, all he felt was the crushing weight of responsibilities and the gnawing pressure to constantly prove himself. The dream he had chased for so long felt distant, obscured by the endless grind of corporate life.

His phone buzzed, pulling him from his thoughts. He glanced at the screen and saw Sahil's name. A small smile tugged at his lips as he answered.

"Hey, Sahil," he said, his voice tired but warm. "How's it going?"

There was a pause on the line, and when Sahil spoke, his frustration was palpable. "It's been rough, Aniket. The latest batch of chargers didn't work—again. I don't know what I'm doing wrong."

Aniket's heart sank with sympathy. "I'm sorry, Sahil. I know how much effort you've put into this."

Sahil sighed, the exhaustion in his voice unmistakable. "Yeah, but it's like every time I think I've got it figured out, something else falls apart. I don't know how much more of this I can take."

Aniket leaned back in his chair, staring blankly at the ceiling. "That's the nature of innovation, Sahil. You're doing something new, and that means hitting walls. But that doesn't mean you should give up."

"I know," Sahil muttered, his frustration simmering just below the surface. "But it's just... hard. I've put everything into this. If I stop now, I don't know if I can start again."

Aniket closed his eyes, the familiar helplessness creeping in. He wanted to comfort his friend, to say something that would ease his burden, but he felt just as trapped in his own struggles. "Maybe you need a break," he offered tentatively. "Step back for a bit. Clear your head."

"I can't afford to take a break," Sahil said sharply. "I've invested everything in this. If I stop now, I'm afraid it'll all slip away."

Aniket swallowed hard, feeling a lump rise in his throat. "I'm sorry, Sahil. I wish I could help more."

There was a moment of silence on the line before Sahil spoke again, his voice softer. "It's okay, Aniket. I just needed to vent."

"I'm always here, Sahil," Aniket replied, his voice quiet but sincere. "You know that."

"Thanks," Sahil said, the gratitude evident in his tone. "And hey, how are things with you? Still surviving the corporate jungle?"

Aniket let out a hollow laugh. "Barely. It's a game, Sahil. And honestly, I don't know if I want to keep playing."

Sahil's voice softened. "Then why are you still there? You don't have to stay if it's killing you."

Aniket's breath caught in his throat. The question was simple, but it struck at the heart of everything he had been wrestling with. Why was he still here? Why was he clinging so tightly to something that seemed to drain him more every day?

"I don't know," he whispered, barely able to say the words. "I guess I'm afraid of what happens if I stop."

"Sometimes," Sahil said gently, "stopping is the bravest thing you can do. You don't have to have all the answers right now, but don't lose yourself in the process."

"I'll try," Aniket whispered, though doubt lingered in his heart.

They spoke for a few more minutes, their conversation eventually turning lighter, filled with the easy banter of two friends who understood each other deeply. But even as they joked, the weight of their respective struggles hung over them, unspoken but very real.

After they hung up, Aniket sat in silence, staring at his computer screen. His life had become a series of survival tactics—navigating office politics, playing the game, ticking the right boxes. But in doing so, he had forgotten what it was like to dream. He had once wanted to change the world, but now, he couldn't even remember what that ambition had felt like.

His phone buzzed again, and he glanced down to see an urgent email from Mr. Sujoy: **URGENT: CLIENT MEETING PREP.** The sight of the subject line filled him with a sudden wave of anger. It was always something, always urgent, always demanding more.

Aniket stared at the message, the frustration rising inside him. He had given so much—his time, his energy, his dreams—and yet, it was never enough. There was always another deadline, another task to prove his worth. But at what cost?

As his hand hovered over the keyboard, he caught sight of Sahil's message: **Don't give up. You've got this.** It was such a small thing, but in that moment, it felt like a lifeline. Aniket took a deep breath, his resolve hardening.

He quickly typed a response to Mr. Sujoy, outlining his plan for the client meeting, his tone professional yet assertive. He was done with being a pawn, done with feeling like a piece of machinery in someone else's game.

After sending the email, Aniket stood up and grabbed his jacket. He needed air, needed to remind himself that there was a world beyond these walls. As he stepped outside into the cool night air, he felt the tension in his body begin to ease. He wandered aimlessly through the city streets, lost in thought, until he found himself at a familiar park—the same one he always went to when he needed to think.

He sat on the bench, head in hands, the enormity of his choices pressing down on him. He didn't know what the future held, but he knew that something had to change. The relentless pursuit of success had come at too high a price.

Just then, he heard footsteps on the path. Looking up, he saw Sahil approaching, a grin on his face.

"I had a feeling you'd be here," Sahil said, sitting down next to him. "You okay?"

Aniket shrugged. "I don't know, Sahil. I thought I had everything figured out, but now... I'm not so sure."

"It's okay not to have all the answers," Sahil replied gently. "You'll find your way."

Aniket turned to his friend, his heart swelling with gratitude. "Thanks, Sahil. I don't know what I'd do without you."

They sat there for a while, talking and laughing, the weight on Aniket's chest gradually lifting. He still didn't have all the answers, but for the first time in a long while, he felt a flicker of hope.

He wasn't alone in this fight, and maybe that was enough to get him through. The art of survival wasn't just about enduring—it was about finding the strength to fight, to dream again. And for the first time in a long time, Aniket felt like he was truly alive.

CHAPTER THIRTEEN

The Cost of Complacency

Aniket sat at his desk, the soft glow of the computer screen casting a pale light over his weary face. The usual buzz of the office had faded; most of his colleagues had long since left, eager to escape the cubicles and return to their lives beyond the glass walls of the corporate fortress.

The clock on his monitor read 7:30 p.m. He stared at the spreadsheet on his screen, the rows of data blurring as fatigue pressed heavily on him. Hours of meticulous analysis filled the report he was working on. It was thorough and precise, yet Aniket couldn't shake the nagging feeling of insignificance. Lately, everything seemed to lack meaning.

Leaning back in his chair, he glanced at the framed picture on his desk. It was from his college graduation—his younger self beaming with hope and ambition, certain that he was destined to make an impact. How far he had come from that moment, and yet, sitting here in this silent office, he felt more distant from his dreams than ever.

He had checked every box—stable job, good salary, respectable position. He had climbed the corporate ladder, but with each step, something precious slipped away. The spark that once drove him had been dulled by the routine, by the comfort of a life that looked perfect on the outside but felt hollow within.

Aniket glanced around the empty office. It was comfortable here. Safe. He knew his role and the rules of the game. But that very comfort had become a trap, a gilded cage preventing him from reaching for something more.

With a sigh, he rubbed his tired eyes. He had everything he was supposed to want, everything he had worked hard to achieve. But he couldn't deny the truth anymore—he felt lost.

His phone buzzed, and he saw Sahil's name flash on the screen. A small smile tugged at his lips.

"Hey, Sahil," Aniket said, his voice warm but strained. "What's up?"

"Aniket!" Sahil's voice was bright, full of energy. "Just checking in. How's life as the corporate warrior?"

Aniket laughed softly, though it held a trace of bitterness. "Same old. Reports, meetings, deadlines. You know the drill."

Sahil chuckled. "Yeah, I remember that grind. But at least you're making the big bucks, right?"

Aniket's gaze flicked to the framed certificates and awards on the wall, symbols of success that now felt more like reminders of what he had sacrificed. "Yeah, I guess. But sometimes I wonder if it's all worth it."

There was a pause on the other end, and when Sahil spoke again, his tone was thoughtful. "What do you mean?"

Aniket sighed, looking out at the darkened windows. "I feel stuck, Sahil. Trapped in this life that's comfortable, sure, but stagnant. I have everything I thought I wanted, but none of it makes me happy."

Sahil's voice softened. "I get that, Aniket. It's easy to chase what we're told to. But if it's not making you happy, then what's the point?"

Aniket leaned forward, resting his elbows on the desk, his head in his hands. "I don't know. I've spent so long building this life, but it feels like I'm living someone else's dream."

Sahil's voice was gentle. "It's not too late, Aniket. You can still choose a different path."

Aniket shook his head, a hollow laugh escaping him. "It's not that simple, Sahil. I have responsibilities, obligations. I can't just walk away."

"I'm not saying you should," Sahil replied quietly. "But maybe it's time to start looking for what makes you happy. It doesn't have to be a big change. Just something that makes you feel alive again."

Aniket closed his eyes, the weight of Sahil's words sinking in. Somewhere along the way, he had lost sight of what made him happy.

"What about you?" Aniket asked after a moment. "How's everything going on your end?"

Sahil hesitated, then spoke with a mix of frustration and resolve. "It's been tough. The business is struggling. I've made a lot of mistakes, and the money's tight. But I'm learning. I'm growing. And for the first time, I feel like I'm doing something that matters."

Aniket felt a pang of envy. Despite the setbacks, Sahil had found something real, something he believed in. He had chosen the harder, uncertain path, but it was his own.

"I'm proud of you, Sahil," Aniket said quietly. "I know it hasn't been easy, but you're doing something incredible."

"Thanks, Aniket," Sahil replied, his voice warm. "And hey, you can do it too. Whatever you're looking for, you can find it. I believe in you."

Aniket nodded, his throat tightening with emotion. "Thanks, Sahil. That means a lot."

They spoke for a while longer, reminiscing about old times, discussing hopes for the future. But the undercurrent of Aniket's discontent lingered, unspoken but palpable.

After they hung up, Aniket remained at his desk, staring out at the city beyond the office windows. Sahil was right. He didn't have to be trapped in this life. But the thought of stepping away from the comfort and stability he had built filled him with an unnamed fear.

He rose slowly, walking over to the windows. The city sprawled out before him, a sea of lights and shadows. He had always admired this view, but tonight it felt distant, as if the world beyond those glass panes was moving without him.

The door to the office clicked open, and Aniket turned to see Meera entering with a stack of files. She looked surprised to find him still there.

"Aniket? I didn't realize you were still working."

He forced a smile. "Yeah, just finishing up."

She set the files on her desk, her brow furrowing with concern. "You're always here late. You should go home, get some rest."

"I will," he said, though he didn't move. "Just a few more things to wrap up."

Meera hesitated, then walked over, her voice soft. "Are you okay? You've seemed... off lately."

Aniket shrugged, staring down at his hands. "I'm fine. Just... tired."

She studied him for a moment, then asked gently, "How did you get through it?"

He blinked, caught off guard. "Through what?"

Meera smiled sadly. "The feeling of being stuck. Going through the motions but not really living."

Aniket looked away. "I don't know."

She stepped closer, her tone encouraging. "You're not alone, Aniket. I went through something similar. It's hard, but the first step is realizing you can change it. Start small. Find something outside of work that makes you feel alive. It won't fix everything overnight, but it helps."

Her words struck a chord in him. He had become so consumed by work that he had forgotten there was more to life. More to him. He had let the job define him, but it didn't have to.

"Thanks, Meera," he said, his voice sincere. "I needed to hear that."

She nodded, offering a supportive smile. "Take care of yourself, Aniket. You're more than this job."

As she walked away, her words echoed in his mind. He was more than his job. He had forgotten that, lost in the illusion of success. But now, standing in the quiet office, he realized he didn't have to be trapped.

Turning back to the window, his heart stirred with a quiet determination. He didn't know what the future held, didn't know how to break free just yet, but he wasn't going to let fear keep him from trying. He would start small, just as Meera had said. He would find something that brought him joy, that made him feel alive again.

For the first time in a long while, he felt a spark of hope. The cost of complacency was too high, and he wasn't willing to pay it anymore.

As he stood there, the city stretched out before him, alive with possibility. Aniket knew he was ready to take the risk, to find his own path.

And for the first time, he felt free.

CHAPTER FOURTEEN

Crisis of Identity

The early morning light barely crept over the horizon as Aniket stared into the bathroom mirror. The reflection looking back at him seemed almost foreign—deep lines around his eyes, an expression weighed down by weariness. He splashed cold water on his face, hoping to clear away the exhaustion that clung to him, but it did little to ease the emptiness growing inside him.

He glanced at his watch; time marched forward relentlessly. He knew he had to get to the office soon, prepare for another day filled with meetings and the relentless grind. Yet, the thought of returning to the same mind-numbing routine filled him with dread.

In the bedroom, his neatly pressed suit hung in the wooden cabinet, a symbol of everything he had worked so hard for. But as he looked at it now, he felt strangely disconnected, as though the person who once wore it with pride was someone else entirely.

Slowly, he dressed, each movement mechanical, his mind adrift. Thoughts of the meeting with Mr. Sujoy later that morning stirred unease in him. There was always pressure to perform, to prove himself, but lately, the weight of those expectations had begun to feel unbearable, like standing at the edge of an unseen precipice.

Grabbing his briefcase, he stepped out into the cool morning air. The familiar heft of the case felt grounding, an anchor to the reality of the life he had built. As he drove to the office through still-quiet streets, he wrestled with an undercurrent of fear—fear that something within him had irrevocably shifted.

Entering the building, Aniket felt a foreboding chill. The tall structure, looming and unyielding, seemed to close in on him as he rode the elevator. When he reached his floor, the usual soft hum of the air conditioning and muted voices greeted him. Nodding at a few colleagues, he moved to his cubicle, eyes glazed over with an exhaustion that went deeper than lack of sleep.

He sat at his desk, staring at the stack of files waiting for him. The sight of them, thick with reports and endless data, turned his stomach. Once, he had found pride in this work, a sense of accomplishment in every project completed. Now, it felt like a burden, a heavy yoke he no longer had the strength to carry.

He opened the first file, flipping through the pages, but the words were a blur of meaningless jargon. Frustrated, he shut it and leaned back, his mind swirling with doubts and confusion. The life he had built—everything he had sacrificed for—suddenly felt hollow, empty.

His phone buzzed, pulling him from his thoughts. He glanced down, his heart lifting slightly at the sight of Sahil's name.

"Hey, Sahil," Aniket answered, trying to sound upbeat, though his voice betrayed his weariness. "What's going on?"

There was a brief silence before Sahil spoke, his tone heavy with worry. "Aniket, I'm in a bit of trouble. The business... it's not going well. Cash flow issues, bad decisions. I don't know how much longer I can keep going."

Aniket's concern for his friend momentarily displaced his own struggles. "What happened?"

Sahil sighed. "Expenses are piling up. I thought I could manage, but it's slipping away from me. I hate to ask, but I might need a loan, just to get through this rough patch."

Aniket's mind raced. He wanted to help—Sahil was his closest friend—but the weight of his own uncertainties bore down on him. "Of course, Sahil. I'll help however I can."

The relief in Sahil's voice was palpable. "I promise, I'll pay you back. I just need a little time."

"I know you will," Aniket replied softly. "We'll figure it out together."

They talked for a few more minutes, their usual light-hearted banter barely concealing the tension of their shared struggles. After they hung up, Aniket sat in silence, torn between his desire to support Sahil and his growing sense of personal despair. He had always been the reliable one, the strong one, but now he felt like he was coming undone.

The hours dragged on. Meetings came and went in a blur, and Aniket found himself operating on autopilot—responding to emails, reviewing reports, attending conference calls. But inside, his mind was racing, caught in an endless loop of questions and fears.

By late afternoon, Aniket found himself standing outside Mr. Sujoy's office, his hand hovering over the door handle. He had been called in for a performance review, a routine meeting that now felt like a moment of reckoning. His heart pounded in his chest as he knocked.

"Come in," Mr. Sujoy's voice called, sharp and businesslike.

Aniket stepped inside, nerves tightening as he approached the desk. Mr. Sujoy looked up from his paperwork, his expression unreadable.

"Ah, Aniket. Have a seat," he said, gesturing to the chair across from him.

Aniket sat, clasping his hands together tightly, trying to steady himself. He felt like a child called into the principal's office, anxiety coiling in his gut.

"I've been reviewing your performance," Mr. Sujoy began, his voice level but direct. "You've done excellent work, but I've noticed a decline in your output recently. Is everything all right?"

Aniket hesitated. The words were on the tip of his tongue, but admitting his struggles felt like an admission of defeat. "I've been finding it difficult to stay motivated," he said quietly.

Sujoy's eyes narrowed in thought. "This job comes with its pressures, Aniket. But you've always handled them well. What's changed?"

The question hung in the air, and Aniket felt the weight of it pressing down on him. His pulse quickened, and he felt as though he was teetering on the edge of a life-altering decision. He thought of Sahil's courage, his willingness to take risks, even when things were falling apart.

"I don't know if this is what I want anymore," he admitted, his voice barely audible.

Sujoy raised an eyebrow, a hint of curiosity flickering in his eyes. "Go on."

Aniket took a deep breath, steadying himself. "I've built my career around this job, around being successful here. But somewhere along the way, I lost myself. I'm not happy, sir. I haven't been happy for a long time."

The silence that followed was deafening. Sujoy studied Aniket for a long moment before leaning back in his chair. "You're a valuable asset to this company, Aniket. But if you're not satisfied, then perhaps it's time to reevaluate what you want."

Aniket nodded, the truth of those words settling heavily on him. For so long, he had been afraid to let go, terrified of losing everything he had worked for. But now, he realized that in holding on so tightly, he had already lost himself.

"Thank you, sir," he said softly, a quiet resolve taking hold. "I appreciate your understanding."

Sujoy nodded. "Take the time you need, Aniket. And when you're ready, we'll talk."

As Aniket left the office, his legs felt unsteady, but a strange sense of relief washed over him. He had taken the first step; one he had been avoiding for too long.

Stepping out into the cool evening air, he felt lighter, as though a weight he had carried for years had finally been lifted. He thought of Sahil, of his friend's resilience, and of the courage it took to face one's fears head-on.

Pulling out his phone, Aniket dialled Sahil's number.

"Hey, Sahil," he began, his voice steady. "I've been thinking... maybe it's time I took a risk too."

There was a pause, and then Sahil's voice came through, filled with cautious hope. "What are you saying?"

"I'm done living a life that doesn't make me happy," Aniket said, conviction rising. "I don't know what's next, but I'm ready to find out."

Sahil's laugh was soft, filled with warmth. "I'm proud of you, Aniket. It's not easy, but I'm here for you. Whatever you need."

Aniket smiled, his heart swelling with gratitude. "Thank you, Sahil. I don't know what I'd do without you."

"Anytime, Aniket," Sahil replied. "We're in this together."

As Aniket hung up, a renewed sense of purpose filled him. The crisis of identity had shaken him to his core, but it had also given him the clarity and courage to break free, to forge his own path.

Walking through the city streets, the lights glowing brightly around him, he knew that while the future was uncertain, he was ready to face it.

He was no longer afraid.

CHAPTER FIFTEEN

The Road Less Travelled

Aniket stood by the window of his office, looking out at the sprawling cityscape below. What once filled him with pride and ambition now seemed distant and hollow. The towering buildings, symbols of achievement and success, stretched endlessly across the horizon, but they no longer inspired him. Instead, he felt a growing detachment, as though he was watching the world unfold from behind a glass wall.

His mind churned with thoughts, tangled in doubt and uncertainty. The recent conversation with Mr. Sujoy had shaken him deeply. It had forced him to confront a truth he had been avoiding for so long: he wasn't happy. From the outside, his life appeared perfect—stable job, impressive career, financial security. But on the inside, everything felt like it was crumbling.

He turned away from the window, his eyes falling on the clutter of files and papers scattered across his desk. The weight of responsibility pressed down on him, suffocating. The thought of walking away from it all—leaving behind the stability he had worked so hard to achieve—was both terrifying and strangely freeing.

Aniket sank into his chair, burying his head in his hands. The same questions circled in his mind like vultures. What if he left? What if he gave up everything he had built? Where would he go? What would he do? The fear of the unknown gnawed at him relentlessly, whispering worst-case scenarios at every turn.

Without thinking, he reached for his phone and scrolled through his contacts until he found Sahil's name. His finger hovered over the call button, his heart racing. He needed to talk to someone—someone who wasn't caught up in the corporate maze, someone who could remind him that there was life beyond the walls of the office.

He pressed the button and held his breath as the phone rang. Each second stretched out, but finally, Sahil's voice came through, bright and warm, like a beacon cutting through the fog in Aniket's mind.

"Aniket! Hey, man! How's it going?"

Aniket swallowed; his throat tight. "Hey, Sahil. I... I needed to talk."

Sahil's tone shifted, filled with concern. "What's going on, man? You don't sound like yourself."

Aniket let out a strained laugh. "Yeah, I guess you could say that. I've been thinking about everything—my job, my life. I just don't know what to do."

There was a pause, then Sahil's voice came, calm and steady. "You're thinking about leaving, aren't you?"

Aniket's heart skipped a beat. The truth was out there now, no longer something he could avoid. "Yeah, I am. But it's not that simple. I've built my whole life around this job. If I leave, I'm throwing it all away."

Sahil sighed on the other end of the line, a sound of empathy. "I know it's scary, Aniket. Leaving something that feels safe, even if it's making you miserable, is the hardest thing to do. But sometimes, you have to trust that there's something better waiting for you."

Aniket leaned back in his chair, staring at the ceiling as he processed his friend's words. "What if I fail, Sahil? What if I leave and everything falls apart?"

Sahil chuckled softly, his tone reassuring. "Then you get back up and try again. Failure isn't the end of the road—it's part of the journey. You'll be okay."

Aniket closed his eyes. Sahil's optimism was something he had always admired. "How did you do it, Sahil?" he asked quietly. "How did you walk away and start over?"

"I didn't have much choice," Sahil admitted. "I was at rock bottom. The only way left was up. But you don't have to wait until things are that bad. You can make the decision now, while you still have your strength and passion. It's not easy, but it's worth it."

Aniket felt a lump rise in his throat. Sahil was right. He had been holding on to a life that no longer made sense, paralyzed by fear of failure. But in reality, he was already failing—failing himself.

"Thanks, Sahil," Aniket said softly. "I don't know if I'm ready, but I think I need to do this."

"You don't have to be ready," Sahil replied with a light laugh. "You just have to be brave. And I know you are. Whatever happens, I'm here for you."

They spoke for a while longer, their conversation moving to lighter topics, shared memories, and the dreams they used to have. But beneath the banter was the quiet understanding that Aniket was standing at a crossroads, facing a decision that could change everything.

After they hung up, Aniket sat in the quiet of his office, staring at the empty space around him. He felt a strange mix of fear and excitement, like standing at the edge of a cliff and knowing that jumping might be the only way forward. The life he had built was safe, predictable, but it was no longer the life he wanted.

He stood and walked back to the window. The city stretched out before him, a sea of lights and possibilities. He pressed his forehead against the cool glass, taking a deep breath as he stared out at the world beyond.

He knew what he had to do. He couldn't keep living this way—trapped in a cycle of fear and complacency. But taking that first step felt like stepping into the unknown, without any guarantees of what might come next.

Aniket took another deep breath, feeling his heart pound in his chest. He wasn't ready, not fully. But maybe he didn't need to be. Maybe, as Sahil had said, all he needed was to be brave.

The thought brought a calm that steadied his racing thoughts. He turned from the window, his mind made up. Tomorrow, he would talk to Mr. Sujoy. He would take that first step, no matter how uncertain the road ahead seemed.

But for now, he needed to get out of the office. He needed fresh air, to clear his mind. Grabbing his jacket, Aniket walked out of the office, the silence of the empty building echoing around him as he made his way to the elevator.

The night air was cool as he stepped outside, the city alive with the sounds of traffic and distant laughter. He took a deep breath, his heart steady, and began walking, letting his feet carry him away from the familiar and into the unknown.

Across the city, Sahil stood in his small workshop, his hands greasy and stained as he put the final pieces of his latest project together. The hum of machinery filled the room, along with the smell of metal and sweat—proof of the countless hours he had poured into his work, chasing a dream that always felt just out of reach.

He stepped back from the small machine he had built, wiping his brow as he admired the simple tool in front of him. It wasn't much, just a crude device designed to make repairs more efficient. But it was his creation—something he had built from the ground up. That thought filled him with a sense of accomplishment, a pride he hadn't felt in a long time.

The workshop was chaotic, filled with scattered tools, unfinished projects, and sketches taped to the walls. But it was his space, his sanctuary. Sahil had built this world for himself, one piece at a time, and now he was ready to take the next step.

He pulled out his phone and saw a message from Rohan, one of his partners in a new venture. The words brought a smile to Sahil's face: *"We're all set for tomorrow. Let's do this!"*

Sahil's heart raced with excitement. The risks ahead were real, and there were no guarantees of success. But for the first time in years, he felt alive. He typed a quick reply: *"I'll be there. Let's make it happen."*

As he shut off the lights in the workshop, Sahil stood in the darkness for a moment, breathing in the silence. The road ahead was uncertain, filled with challenges he couldn't yet see, but he knew one thing: he was ready. Ready to embrace the unknown, to take the road less travelled, and to build something real.

And as he stepped into the cool night, he knew Aniket was ready too.

They were both standing at the edge of something vast and uncharted. The road less travelled was calling—and for the first time, they were both ready to answer.

The Illusion of Stability

The office buzzed with excitement as news of Aniket's promotion spread like wildfire. Congratulations poured in from every corner—emails, handshakes, nods of approval in the hallway. His colleagues, their faces glowing with admiration, stopped by his new corner office one by one.

"Congratulations, Aniket! You've earned it!"

"About time they recognized your hard work!"

"Next stop, the executive suite, right?"

Aniket smiled, offering polite thanks as his responses became mechanical. "Thank you, I appreciate it." Each phrase felt rehearsed, hollow. As the day wore on, the handshakes and words of praise blended, offering little satisfaction. Despite the smiles and pats on the back, a gnawing emptiness settled deep within him.

Sitting at his desk, Aniket stared at the congratulatory email from Mr. Sujoy, officially announcing his new title: *Senior Project Manager*. The promotion he had worked toward for years had finally arrived, along with a sizable raise, a larger office, and more responsibilities. Yet, none of it brought the fulfilment he had imagined. Instead, a profound sense of loss swept over him.

His eyes drifted to the expansive windows that offered a sweeping view of the city skyline. It was a view that many would envy, a symbol of success. But to Aniket, it seemed distant, almost mocking. He had spent years chasing this achievement, sacrificing time, relationships, and parts of himself along the way. And now, as he looked out over the city, he couldn't shake the feeling that something important had been left behind.

He turned back to his desk, scanning the words in Mr. Sujoy's email again, but the corporate platitudes felt meaningless. Words like *hard work, dedication,* and *contributions to growth* no longer held the power they once had. It was all part of a game he had mastered, but one that he no longer wanted to play.

His phone buzzed, and his heart lifted slightly when he saw Sahil's name on the screen.

"Hey, Sahil," Aniket said, his voice carrying a weariness he couldn't quite hide. "Guess what?"

Sahil's laugh came through, warm and full of life. "Let me guess... you got the promotion?"

Aniket smiled, though it felt forced. "Yeah, I did."

"That's awesome, Aniket! Congratulations!" Sahil's voice was filled with genuine excitement, the kind of enthusiasm Aniket wished he could share.

"Thanks," Aniket replied softly, his eyes drifting back to the email. "But... I don't know, Sahil. It doesn't feel like I thought it would."

There was a brief pause before Sahil spoke again, this time more serious. "What do you mean?"

Aniket sighed, running a hand through his hair. "I thought this promotion would make me feel... fulfilled. But now that I have it, it feels empty. Like I've been chasing something that doesn't even matter."

Sahil's voice was calm, filled with understanding. "You're not alone, Aniket. A lot of people think success will bring happiness, but when they get there, it's not what they expected."

Aniket leaned back in his chair, staring up at the ceiling. "Yeah, but what do I do now? I've spent my whole life working toward this. If this isn't what I want... then what is?"

Sahil's tone softened. "Maybe it's time to start looking for something that makes you feel alive again. It doesn't have to be a huge change, just small steps. What used to make you happy, Aniket? What did you love before this job consumed everything?"

Aniket closed his eyes, trying to recall the last time he felt genuine joy. He remembered his old hobbies—reading, painting, writing—but they felt like distant memories. He couldn't remember the last time he did something just for himself, something that wasn't tied to work or success.

"I don't know, Sahil," he said quietly. "I feel like I've lost myself somewhere along the way."

Sahil sighed; empathy heavy in his voice. "I get it. But you can find yourself again. It's not too late. Just take it one step at a time. And remember, I'm here for you."

Aniket felt a lump rise in his throat. He didn't realize how much he needed to hear those words. "Thanks, Sahil. I don't know what I'd do without you."

"Anytime, Aniket. And hey, if you ever want to take a break from the corporate world, the workshop's always open. It's not as glamorous as your office, but it's real, and that's what matters."

Aniket laughed softly, the tension in his chest easing a little. "I might take you up on that."

They talked for a few more minutes, sharing light-hearted banter, but beneath the laughter, Aniket's unease lingered, like a shadow that refused to leave.

After hanging up, Aniket sat in his chair, staring at the sleek modern furniture in his office, the framed certificates on the wall, the skyline outside the window. Everything looked perfect, yet nothing felt right. The promotion, the recognition, the success—it all felt like a façade, a mask covering up a deeper truth he didn't want to face.

He stood and walked to the window. The bustling city below seemed alive with energy, but to Aniket, it looked like a graveyard of forgotten dreams. He pressed his forehead against the glass, the cool surface grounding him. He had spent so many years striving to climb the corporate ladder, but now that he was at the top, the view was bleak.

Aniket turned back toward his desk, where a stack of reports awaited his attention. The thought of diving back into those numbers filled him with dread. It was as if each file, each spreadsheet, represented a piece of his soul he had sold for success.

The hours dragged on, filled with meetings and emails, but his heart wasn't in it. He performed his duties out of obligation, maintaining the appearance of competence and ambition, but inside, he was a mess of confusion and doubt.

By the end of the day, he felt drained—emotionally, mentally, and physically. Gathering his belongings, he left the office and stepped out into the cool evening air. The city hummed with life around him, but all Aniket felt was a growing desire to escape. To run away from the demands of a life that no longer felt like his own.

He pulled out his phone and dialled Sahil's number.

"Hey, Sahil," he said, his voice steady but filled with resolve. "I think I need to take you up on that offer."

Sahil paused for a moment before replying, "You mean the workshop?"

"Yeah," Aniket replied. "I need to start somewhere."

Across the city, Sahil stood in his workshop, a smile tugging at the corners of his mouth as he talked with Aniket and his desire to join him. The workshop was buzzing with energy, a small group of friends and colleagues gathered around a large workbench, discussing their latest project. The hum of machinery and the clatter of tools filled the space, but it was the sense of purpose that permeated the air, a feeling of being part of something meaningful.

Sahil had started small, with just a few ideas and a lot of determination. But now, looking around the workshop, he saw the fruits of their labour slowly taking shape. It wasn't perfect—there were still financial struggles, setbacks, and challenges—but it was real.

He picked up one of the prototypes they had been working on, a tool designed to revolutionize small repairs. It was a simple concept but innovative, practical, and most importantly, theirs. As Sahil turned the device over in his hands, a sense of pride swelled within him. They were building something from the ground up, something that mattered.

He glanced over at his team, his heart filled with gratitude for the people who had believed in his vision. They had taken a risk by joining him, stepping away from more secure paths to pursue something uncertain. But together, they were creating something lasting.

Sahil set the prototype down and looked out the workshop door, where the last rays of the setting sun filtered in. The road ahead was still filled with obstacles, but he felt like he was on the right path.

He quickly typed a message to Aniket:
"You're always welcome here. We'll figure it out together."

Setting his phone aside, Sahil felt a wave of determination wash over him. The journey had only just begun, but the most important part was that they were moving forward. Aniket might still be searching for his path, but Sahil knew they would both find their way. Together, they were building something real, something far more valuable than the illusion of stability.

As Sahil turned back to his team, the clatter of tools and hum of machinery filled the workshop once more. There was still a lot of work ahead, but the road less travelled was proving to be the only one worth taking.

CHAPTER SEVENTEEN

The Fall

The atmosphere in the office was thick with tension. Aniket sat at his desk, staring at his computer screen, unable to shake the growing sense of dread gnawing at him. The subject line of the email that had just popped up was brief but carried an ominous weight: *Company Announcement: Restructuring Plan.*

The rumours had been circulating for weeks—subtle, whispered conversations in the break room, uneasy glances exchanged in the hallways—but now it was real. The restructuring plan had finally arrived, and the unsettling calm before the storm was about to break. Aniket clicked on the email, his fingers trembling slightly as he scrolled through the message, scanning for clues about what it might mean for him and his colleagues.

Words like *streamlining operations* and *organizational realignment* jumped out at him, each phrase carefully crafted to sound efficient and necessary. But to Aniket, they felt like a death knell. He knew what was coming. Layoffs. Job cuts. The kind of "realignment" that left people suddenly, painfully unemployed.

He leaned back in his chair, his heart pounding, his mind racing as the full weight of the situation settled over him. The promotion he had recently received was supposed to bring security, a sense of stability. But now, with just one email, it all felt fragile, like everything he had worked for was slipping through his fingers. The sensation was dizzying, like standing on the edge of a cliff with nothing solid beneath him.

The usual office buzz had shifted, replaced by an undercurrent of anxiety. Small groups of colleagues gathered near doorways and by their desks, whispering with worried expressions. Aniket could see the fear in their eyes, and it mirrored his own. No one knew who would be affected or how deep the cuts would go, but everyone could sense that something significant was coming.

He glanced at the calendar on his desk, noticing the town hall meeting scheduled for later that afternoon. It was supposed to be an opportunity for senior management to provide "clarity" on the restructuring plan, but Aniket knew better. It wasn't about clarity; it was about damage control. The company was bracing for impact, and the town hall was their attempt to manage the panic before it spread like wildfire.

His phone buzzed, and he picked it up, his chest tightening when he saw Sahil's name. The one person who could always ground him in moments of chaos.

"Hey, Aniket," Sahil's voice came through, cautious but warm. "You alright?"

Aniket sighed, leaning back in his chair. "I don't know, Sahil. They're restructuring the company. I just got the email."

There was a pause, and then Sahil's voice softened with concern. "I'm sorry, man. I know how much this job means to you. I know you've put everything into it."

"Yeah, but now I'm starting to wonder if it was worth it. I've given so much to this place, and for what? I might lose it all anyway."

Sahil was quiet for a moment, and when he spoke again, his voice was steady, filled with the calm that Aniket so desperately needed. "You're not going to lose everything, Aniket. No matter what happens, you're going to get through this. You've always figured things out. And remember, my workshop is always open for you, no matter what."

Aniket felt a lump form in his throat, the kindness in Sahil's words hitting him harder than he expected. "Thanks, Sahil. I just... I don't know how to deal with this."

"We'll figure it out together," Sahil said gently. "Whatever happens, you're not alone."

After a few more minutes of conversation, they hung up. Aniket sat in the quiet of his office, his thoughts swirling as he watched his colleagues move about the room, their faces lined with the same fear and uncertainty. The fragility of everything he had built suddenly felt overwhelming.

He stood up, needing to escape the oppressive atmosphere, and walked to the break room. As he poured himself a cup of coffee, he overheard snippets of conversation behind him—voices low but charged with anxiety.

"They're cutting the entire marketing department."

"Yeah, I heard they're outsourcing IT too. We're all screwed."

"I don't know how we're supposed to manage if half the team is gone..."

The voices quieted as Aniket turned, catching the worried glances from his coworkers. They offered small, sympathetic smiles, but he could see their fear—fear that mirrored his own.

Back at his desk, Aniket's mind refused to settle. He tried to lose himself in work, but the words on the screen blurred into a jumble of numbers and meaningless phrases. His focus was shattered by the weight of what was coming.

Finally, the hour for the town hall meeting arrived. Aniket's legs felt weak as he made his way to the large conference room, where dozens of employees were already seated, their faces tense with expectation. He sat near the back, trying to steady his breath as Mr. Sujoy, the senior manager, entered the room. His face, as always, was unreadable, the perfect mask of corporate professionalism.

"Thank you all for coming," Mr. Sujoy began, his voice calm and controlled, as if he wasn't about to turn lives upside down. "I know this is a difficult time for everyone, and I want to reassure you that we are committed to making this transition as smooth as possible."

Aniket felt anger rise in his chest. *Smooth as possible?* Easy for him to say, sitting in his executive office, unaffected by the cuts and layoffs. He tuned out as Mr. Sujoy continued, spouting corporate jargon about streamlining operations and ensuring long-term sustainability. It all felt like a performance, an attempt to manage the chaos without truly addressing the human cost.

"...as part of the restructuring, we will be reducing our workforce by approximately 15%," Mr. Sujoy said, his voice sombre but detached. "Impacted departments will be notified individually, and those affected will receive severance packages along with support during this transition."

Aniket's stomach dropped. Fifteen percent. That was a massive cut. He glanced around the room, seeing the same realization dawning on his colleagues' faces. Some of them wouldn't be here tomorrow. People he had worked with for years—some of them friends—would lose their jobs, their livelihoods, in a matter of days.

When the meeting ended, Aniket felt like he was moving through a haze. His legs were shaky as he left the conference room, the buzz of anxious voices surrounding him. People gathered in small groups, talking in low, tense whispers, trying to figure out what was coming next.

Back at his desk, Aniket stared at the computer screen. The earlier email about the restructuring was still open, but the words seemed meaningless now. He had survived—at least for the moment—but it didn't feel like a victory. It felt hollow, like everything he had worked for was crumbling around him. He had survived, but at what cost?

Across the city, in his small workshop, Sahil stared at the letter in his hands, the bold print of the words *Notice of Termination* searing into his mind. The landlord was giving them thirty days to vacate the premises, citing noise complaints and unauthorized modifications to the space. It was a crushing blow, one that he hadn't seen coming.

Around him, his small team of friends and colleagues stood in stunned silence, their faces filled with disbelief. They had worked so hard to build this workshop, pouring every ounce of energy into it, and now it was being ripped away from them.

"What are we going to do, Sahil?" Rohan's voice was tight with panic. "We don't have the money to move. We're barely scraping by as it is."

Sahil took a deep breath, trying to stay calm. "We'll figure something out," he said, though his hands were trembling. "We've faced worse than this. We'll find a way."

"But how?" Priya, one of the engineers, asked, her voice shaking. "We don't have anywhere else to go. If we lose this place..."

Sahil forced a steadying breath, his mind racing. They had come so far, had fought so hard to make this dream a reality. They couldn't give up now.

"We'll downsize if we have to. Work from home, rent a smaller space. But we're not giving up," he said, his voice stronger now. "We've worked too hard for this."

The team nodded, though their faces were still filled with uncertainty. Sahil knew they trusted him, believed in him, but the pressure was overwhelming. He had to find a solution, and fast. Thirty days wasn't much time.

After the team dispersed, Sahil sat alone in the workshop, staring at the letter in his hands. His heart ached with the weight of it all. He had promised his team they would get through this, but now, sitting in the quiet, he wasn't sure. The pressure was crushing him.

He pulled out his phone and dialled Aniket's number, hoping his friend's voice would give him some comfort.

"Hey, Sahil," Aniket answered, sounding tired and worn out. "What's going on?"

Sahil swallowed hard, his voice breaking as he explained the situation. "We're losing the workshop. They're kicking us out."

"What?" Aniket's shock was palpable. "Why?"

Sahil explained, feeling the weight of it all as he spoke. "I don't know what we're going to do, Aniket. We don't have the money to move, and I can't let my team down."

There was a pause, and then Aniket's voice came through, filled with quiet confidence. "You'll figure it out, Sahil. You always do. And whatever you need, I'm here."

Sahil felt a tear slip down his cheek, his chest tightening with emotion. "Thanks, Aniket. I don't want to let them down."

"You won't," Aniket said. "You're stronger than you think. We'll figure this out."

As they ended the call, Sahil felt a small spark of determination reignite in his chest. They were both facing uncertainty, both standing on the edge of the unknown. But the fall wasn't the end. It was the beginning.

And together, they would rise again.

The Rise of the Underdog

The sound of machinery echoed through the small workshop, creating a steady rhythm that Sahil had come to appreciate. He stood in the middle of it all, his hands skilfully working over a small motor, his face streaked with grease and sweat. Around him, his team was hard at work, their focused expressions mirroring his own. Despite the exhaustion, there was an unmistakable sense of energy in the air—an intensity driven by their shared determination.

After losing the lease on their original workshop, Sahil and his team had scrambled to find a new space. Weeks were spent knocking on doors, following leads, and negotiating impossible rents on a shoestring budget. Every potential place seemed out of reach, and frustration began to creep in, but Sahil held fast to one principle: "God helps those who refuse to give up." This belief was the thread that kept them going, even when the path seemed bleak.

One evening, just as Sahil was about to call it a day, his phone rang. It was a distant relative; someone he hadn't spoken to in years. During their casual conversation, Sahil mentioned his predicament, and to his surprise, the relative offered a glimmer of hope—an old, unused garage on the outskirts of the city. It was rundown, hardly ideal, but the rent was within their budget. Intrigued, Sahil decided to visit the next day.

The garage was far from perfect. Small, cluttered, and in desperate need of a deep clean, the space barely resembled a workshop. But where others saw problems, Sahil saw potential. He believed that with enough effort—and a bit of divine help—this rundown garage could become the heart of their operations. Encouraged by his team and with a little financial support from family and friends, Sahil signed the lease.

The next hurdle was moving. With no money for professional movers, Sahil and his team, joined by family members, rolled up their sleeves and got to work. Over the course of a gruelling weekend, they moved equipment, set up makeshift workstations, and cleaned every inch of the space. Sahil's cousin, an electrician, installed better lighting, and his team of mechanics, helped repair some of the old machinery that had been left behind. Piece by piece, the garage was transformed into a functional workshop.

Still, Sahil knew that simply having a space wasn't enough. They needed innovation to stand out. He had been tinkering with a new method of repairing industrial equipment that could drastically reduce costs. His approach involved modular repair parts and a custom-built diagnostic tool that pinpointed problems with greater accuracy. The idea was simple: quicker repairs, fewer replacement parts, and lower costs for clients.

They started by testing this method on equipment owned by friends and family. Sahil's uncle, whose small business was struggling with frequent machinery breakdowns, became their first test case. Using their new technique, Sahil and his team repaired the machinery faster than any previous service, reducing the costs by nearly half. The success was undeniable, and word began to spread.

At first, it was slow—just a few local businesses, curious to try a new service. But soon, their reputation for innovation and affordability grew. More clients began calling, drawn by the promise of reliable repairs at a fraction of the usual cost. What had started as a desperate attempt to keep their business afloat was now transforming into a thriving enterprise.

The team expanded as well. With the increasing demand, they brought on new employees, each one referred by someone who had seen their work firsthand. The workshop, once a cramped and cluttered garage, now buzzed with life. They found new ways to streamline operations, further reducing costs while maintaining quality.

One day, as Sahil wiped the sweat from his brow, watching his team work on their largest order yet—twenty custom-made motors for a local manufacturing company—he felt a deep sense of pride. This project, their biggest break so far, had come about unexpectedly. Sahil had met the company's owner at a community event and pitched their services with nothing but hope. To his surprise, the owner had been impressed, and now, they were fulfilling an order that could take their business to the next level.

"Hey, Sahil!" Rohan's excited voice cut through the noise. He waved a piece of paper in the air, his face flushed with exhilaration. "You're not going to believe this!"

Sahil looked up, wiping his hands on a rag. "What is it?"

Rohan rushed over, barely able to contain his excitement. "We just got an email from *Innovate Today*. They want to feature us in their next issue!"

Sahil's eyes widened in disbelief. *Innovate Today* was a highly respected tech magazine known for spotlighting innovative startups and breakthrough ideas. A feature in their publication could mean new clients, exposure, and a chance to scale their business beyond anything they had imagined.

"Are you serious?" Sahil's voice was barely a whisper, the weight of the news sinking in.

Rohan nodded eagerly. "Completely serious! They said they've heard about our work and want to interview you next week."

For a moment, Sahil was speechless. He had never imagined that their scrappy little operation would attract this kind of attention. It felt surreal, like a dream he was afraid to wake up from. "That's... incredible," he finally said, his voice trembling with emotion. "I don't even know what to say."

"You don't have to say anything, boss," Priya called from across the workshop, grinning. "Just keep doing what you're doing. We're all behind you."

Sahil nodded, his chest swelling with gratitude as he looked around at his team. These were the people who had believed in him, who had worked beside him through every setback, every failure. This victory wasn't his alone—it belonged to all of them. They had built this together.

"Alright, everyone," Sahil said, regaining his composure. "We've got a lot of work to do before that interview. Let's show them what we're made of."

A cheer went up around the workshop, and the team dove back into their tasks with renewed energy. As Sahil watched them work, a deep sense of purpose settled over him. This was what they had been working for, what they had fought for. They were finally breaking through.

Across the city, Aniket sat in his cubicle, staring blankly at his computer screen. He was supposed to be finishing a report on the company's quarterly results, but his thoughts kept drifting elsewhere. His phone lay on the desk beside him, a message from Sahil opens on the screen. It was a photo of Sahil standing proudly in the middle of his bustling workshop, grinning from ear to ear. The team around him looked tired, their clothes smeared with grease, but their smiles were bright, their eyes filled with excitement.

Aniket felt a pang of envy. Sahil had taken a risk, had stepped out of the safety net to build something from scratch. He was living his dream, doing something that mattered. And Aniket... Aniket was here, stuck in the monotonous grind of corporate life, staring at spreadsheets and reports that felt utterly meaningless.

He glanced around the office, taking in the rows of identical cubicles, the tired faces of his colleagues bent over their workstations. The atmosphere was heavy, drained of the energy it had once held. The recent restructuring had gutted their department, leaving everyone on edge, afraid to speak up or make a mistake. Aniket had survived the layoffs and had even been promoted, but the promotion came with a crushing weight. The expectations were relentless, the pressure suffocating. He had more money, more responsibility, but he felt emptier than ever.

His phone buzzed. It was another message from Sahil: *"You should come by the workshop sometime. I'd love to show you what we've been working on."*

Aniket hesitated, staring at the message. He had been avoiding the workshop, avoiding the reminder of the risks he hadn't taken. But sitting here in the sterile, lifeless office, he felt a sudden surge of determination. Maybe it was time to face it.

"I'll come by this weekend," he replied. *"I'd love to see it."*

That weekend, Aniket found himself standing outside Sahil's workshop. The building was small and tucked away, but he could already sense the energy within. He took a deep breath, his hand hovering over the door handle. He had come this far; there was no turning back now.

As he stepped inside, the workshop buzzed with life. Machinery hummed, and voices filled the space with an infectious energy. It was chaotic but purposeful, every movement contributing to something larger.

"Aniket!" Sahil called out, waving him over. Covered in grease and sweat, Sahil looked exhausted, but his smile was genuine, his eyes alive with excitement.

Aniket couldn't help but smile back. "This place is incredible, Sahil. You've built something amazing."

Sahil grinned, pride shining in his eyes. "Thanks, man. It's been a tough journey, but we're getting there."

As Sahil gave Aniket a tour of the workshop, explaining the projects they were working on and the innovations they had developed, Aniket felt something stir inside him. The passion in Sahil's voice, the sense of purpose in the air—it was everything Aniket had been missing.

"You've done something incredible here," Aniket said softly. "I'm really proud of you."

Sahil's smile softened. "Thanks, Aniket. That means a lot."

As they stood there, surrounded by the sounds of creation, Aniket felt a shift. The safe, predictable life he had built now felt like a cage, while the chaotic, messy world of the workshop seemed filled with possibility. He didn't know if he was ready to take the leap, but now, he felt the courage to consider it.

The rise of the underdog wasn't just about success—it was about resilience, about having the strength to take risks and the determination to keep going in the face of adversity. And as Aniket stood there, watching Sahil and his team bring their ideas to life, he realized that maybe it was time for him to take that risk, to find his own path.

And, finally, he felt ready.

CHAPTER NINETEEN

The Courage to Quit

Aniket sat in his office, the hum of the air conditioning and the distant murmur of voices the only sounds in the otherwise silent room. The blinds were drawn, casting long shadows across the sleek, polished surfaces of his desk. He glanced at the clock on his computer screen—6:45 p.m. The office was nearly empty, most of his colleagues having left hours ago. But he was still here, staring at the email he had been drafting for the past hour, his fingers frozen over the keyboard.

It was a resignation letter. The words were neatly typed and carefully considered, but they felt foreign, like something he had written for someone else. He had read it over and over again, his heart pounding with each line, but he couldn't bring himself to hit send.

Leaning back in his chair, Aniket's gaze shifted to the framed certificates and awards on the wall. They had once symbolized success, markers of his professional achievements and the milestones he'd worked tirelessly to reach. But now, they felt like chains—reminders of a life he had built but no longer recognized as his own.

He closed his eyes, his thoughts swirling with doubts and fears. Quitting—just the word itself sent a shiver down his spine, wrapping him in anxiety. This job had been his identity, his source of stability. Without it, who was he? What would define him if he walked away from everything he'd worked for?

The thought of leaving behind the security of his corporate life terrified him. He had no plan, no roadmap for what came next. All he had was a vague, unsettling yearning for something more—something that would make him feel alive again.

His phone buzzed on the desk, breaking through the silence. He glanced at the screen, his heart lifting slightly when he saw Sahil's name. A message popped up: "Hey, man. Big news. Call me when you can."

Aniket felt a pang of envy. Sahil had always been the brave one—the one who took risks, who followed his gut even when the path ahead was uncertain. And now, Sahil was living out his dreams, expanding his business and chasing new horizons with a courage Aniket couldn't help but admire.

After a brief hesitation, Aniket dialled Sahil's number. The phone rang twice before Sahil's voice came through, brimming with excitement.

"Aniket! I was just about to call you. You're not going to believe what happened today."

Aniket forced a smile. "What's going on, Sahil? You sound like you're about to burst."

Sahil's laugh was full of joy, a kind of joy Aniket hadn't felt in what seemed like ages. "We got an offer from a major distributor! They want to take our product nationwide. This could be a game-changer for us!"

Aniket's eyes widened in disbelief. "Are you serious? That's incredible, Sahil. Congratulations."

"Thanks, man," Sahil said, his voice still buzzing with excitement. "I'm still processing it. There's a lot to figure out, but if we can pull this off... it could be huge."

Aniket leaned back in his chair, feeling both pride for his friend and an unsettling wave of envy. Sahil was stepping into the unknown, moving forward, while Aniket was stuck here, unable to even press send on his resignation letter.

"That's amazing, Sahil," Aniket said softly, his voice betraying a hint of sadness. "I'm really happy for you."

Sahil must have picked up on the tone because his voice shifted, becoming softer and more thoughtful. "What's going on, Aniket? You don't sound okay."

Aniket's eyes moved back to the glowing screen in front of him, where the unsent resignation letter stared back like a daunting challenge. "I've been thinking about quitting, Sahil. But I don't know... I'm scared. I don't know if I can do it."

A long silence followed, and when Sahil finally spoke, his voice was filled with understanding. "It's okay to be scared, Aniket. Quitting isn't easy. It's one of the hardest things you can do. But sometimes, it's the only way to move forward."

Aniket felt his throat tighten, his eyes stinging with unshed tears. "What if I fail, Sahil? What if I walk away and end up with nothing?"

Sahil sighed gently, his tone steady and reassuring. "Failure isn't the end, Aniket. It's part of the process. You have to trust yourself, trust that no matter what happens, you'll find a way."

Aniket's heart ached with indecision. "I wish I could be as brave as you, Sahil. You've always known what you wanted, and you've had the courage to go after it."

Sahil laughed softly, though there was a touch of sadness in his voice. "I'm not as brave as you think. I'm scared all the time. But I've learned that sometimes, you just have to take the leap. Because if you don't, you'll never know what you're capable of."

Aniket stared at the screen, his fingers hovering uncertainly over the keyboard. He thought about all the years he had spent here, the long hours, the countless sacrifices. He had worked so hard to climb the corporate ladder, to achieve success. But now, standing at the peak, all he felt was a deep, hollow emptiness.

"What if I'm not ready?" he asked, his voice barely audible.

"Then take your time," Sahil replied, his voice gentle but firm. "But remember, you're not trapped, Aniket. You always have a choice."

Aniket nodded, even though Sahil couldn't see him. "Thank you, Sahil. I needed to hear that."

"Anytime," Sahil said warmly. "And whatever you decide, I'm here for you."

After they hung up, Aniket sat in the quiet of his office, his mind racing. He felt a strange mix of fear and determination. This was a turning point—one that would define his future.

He glanced at the email again. It was a simple message, yet it held so much weight. He thought about Sahil, about the risks he had taken and the courage it took to follow his heart. Sahil was building something real, something meaningful. Aniket wanted that too. He wanted to feel alive again.

With trembling fingers, Aniket hovered over the send button, his heart pounding in his chest. The fear was still there, but so was a growing sense of determination. He couldn't keep living like this, trapped in a cycle of fear and complacency.

He pressed send.

The email vanished from the screen, a small confirmation box appearing briefly before fading away. Aniket sat back, his heart racing, his hands shaking. He had done it. He had taken the leap.

A wave of panic washed over him, but along with it came an unexpected feeling of relief. The chains that had held him in place for so long were broken, and for the first time in years, he felt free.

He stood up, his legs unsteady, and walked to the window. The city stretched out before him, a sprawling expanse of lights and shadows. It looked different now, filled with possibilities he hadn't seen before. He took a deep breath, his heart beginning to steady.

He had freed himself. He had taken the first step toward reclaiming his life. And now, as he stood on the edge of the unknown, he felt a spark of hope that had long been absent.

The courage to resign had been the hardest thing he had ever done, but it was also the most important. He didn't know what the future held or where this new path would take him, but he felt in control of his own destiny.

As Aniket walked out of the office for the last time, he felt lighter, freer. His mind buzzed with plans, ideas, possibilities. He didn't have all the answers, but that didn't scare him anymore. He was ready to embrace the uncertainty, to face whatever challenges lay ahead.

This was just the beginning. The courage to quit was the first step in finding himself again, in building a life that truly mattered. And as Aniket stepped into the cool night air, he knew one thing for sure: he was ready to take that journey, no matter where it led.

The Breaking Point

Aniket sat slumped at his desk, the walls of his office seemingly closing in around him like a vice. The flickering fluorescent lights overhead cast jagged shadows across the papers scattered across his desk, their constant strobe only adding to the tension gnawing at him. His eyes, red and heavy from sleepless nights, burned with exhaustion, and his head throbbed with a dull pain that no amount of coffee or painkillers could numb.

The sound of a new email notification pinged on his computer, its sharp tone cutting through the silence like a blade. He flinched, his fingers trembling as they reached for the mouse, clumsy and weak from the weight of stress. He opened the email, but the words blurred before his eyes, blending into an incomprehensible mass of demands and deadlines. Another urgent request. Another last-minute change. Another impossible task.

Aniket leaned back in his chair, closing his eyes tightly, trying to block out the overwhelming flood of tasks piling on top of him. His chest tightened with each shallow breath, as if a steel band were wrapped around him, suffocating him slowly. He felt as though he was drowning, dragged beneath the surface by a sea of expectations, with no end in sight.

He had once believed that quitting this job would set him free—that it would release him from the relentless pace, the never-ending demands, and the crushing weight of corporate life. But when he had submitted his resignation, they had begged him to stay just a little longer, to help with the transition. Unable to refuse, he had agreed. And now, here he was—still trapped, still suffocating.

The clock in the corner of his screen blinked 3:45 a.m. The office was deserted, except for the faint hum of the air conditioning and the eerie creaks of the building settling in the quiet of the night. He was alone. Completely alone.

He glanced at the bottle of painkillers on his desk, his hands shaking as he fumbled to open it. He shook out two pills into his palm and swallowed them dry, the bitterness clinging to his throat. He rested his head in his hands, trying to will the tension away, but his mind was a whirl of anxiety and exhaustion. How much longer could he keep this up? How much longer before he broke completely?

A soft knock on the door startled him, and his head snapped up, his vision swimming as he struggled to focus. The door creaked open, and Meera stepped inside, her face pale and drawn, her eyes wide with concern as she took in the sight of him.

"Aniket," she said softly, her voice gentle but urgent. "What are you still doing here?"

He tried to smile, but it felt forced and brittle, as if any moment it might crack. "Just... finishing up some work."

Meera frowned, her eyes narrowing as she stepped closer, her gaze flicking over him—the dark circles under his eyes, the trembling of his hands, the slick sheen of sweat on his forehead. "You look terrible. You need to go home. This isn't healthy."

Aniket shook his head, his voice tight with strain. "I can't, Meera. There's too much to do. If I don't finish this... I don't know what will happen."

She rested a hand on his shoulder, her touch light but steady. "Aniket, this is going to kill you if you keep going like this. No job is worth that."

A surge of anger and frustration bubbled up inside him, his chest tightening as he fought to contain it. "You don't understand," he snapped, his voice sharp and brittle. "I have to do this. I can't let everyone down. I can't fail."

Meera's expression softened; her eyes filled with sadness. "You're not failing, Aniket. You're human. You need to take care of yourself."

He let out a harsh, bitter laugh, the sound hollow and painful. "Human? I feel like a machine. I just keep going and going, doing what I'm told, not feeling anything. I'm so tired, Meera. I don't even know who I am anymore."

Tears welled in her eyes, her voice trembling as she spoke. "Aniket, please. Just take a break. Go home, get some sleep. We'll figure this out together."

He stared at her, his vision blurring as tears he had been holding back for weeks finally spilled over, silent and hot down his cheeks. "I can't," he whispered, his voice breaking. "I don't know how."

Meera took a deep breath, her hand squeezing his shoulder gently. "Then let me help you. You don't have to do this alone."

Aniket nodded slowly, his heart aching with the weight of everything that had brought him to this point. "Okay," he murmured. "I'll try."

With Meera's help, he gathered his things, her movements gentle and careful, as if she were afraid, he might shatter. Numbly, he followed her out of the office, his mind fogged by exhaustion and despair. The quiet of the city streets felt distant, unreal, as they stepped into the cool night air. Everything around him felt detached, as if he were watching himself from a distance.

Meera called a cab, staying by his side until he was seated in the back, her hand resting lightly on his arm. "You're going to be okay, Aniket," she said softly. "We'll get through this."

Aniket closed his eyes as the cab pulled away from the curb, the streetlights blurring into streaks of light as he sank deeper into his exhaustion. He didn't know if Meera was right. He didn't know if he would ever be okay again. But for now, he was too tired to care.

On the other side of the city, Sahil sat in his small office, his heart pounding with a mix of excitement and fear. The contract lay open on the desk in front of him, the words staring up at him like a challenge he wasn't sure he was ready to accept. This was the opportunity they had been waiting for—the chance to take their business to the next level. But it was also a risk, a massive one.

The distributor had offered them a deal that could transform everything. But it required a significant investment, an expansion that would stretch them thin. If it worked, they'd be catapulted into a new league. If it failed... they would lose everything.

He glanced at his team, the group that had been with him through every struggle, every setback. Their faces reflected a blend of hope and anxiety, their eyes on him, waiting for his decision. The weight of their trust, their belief in him, pressed down heavily on his shoulders.

Rohan leaned forward, breaking the silence. "What do you think, Sahil? Can we do this?"

Sahil's hands shook slightly as he ran them through his hair. "I don't know, Rohan. It's a huge risk. We're putting everything on the line."

Priya nodded; her voice quiet but steady. "But if we don't take this chance, we might never get another one. It's a gamble, but it's also an opportunity."

Sahil's eyes drifted back to the contract. He had always been the one to push forward, to take the leap even when the path was unclear. But this was different. The stakes were higher, the risks greater. He felt the familiar fear gnawing at him, whispering all the ways they could fail.

"What if we fail?" he asked quietly, more to himself than to the room.

There was a long pause before Rohan spoke again, his voice calm and certain. "Then we'll get back up and try again. We've made it this far, Sahil. We can't stop now."

Sahil looked around at his team, at the people who had stood by him through every failure, every success. They weren't just colleagues—they were family. And they were counting on him to lead them forward.

Taking a deep breath, Sahil picked up the pen, his hand steady as he signed the contract. "We're doing this," he said, his voice filled with determination. "We're taking the leap."

A cheer erupted around the room, the tension breaking as they celebrated the decision. But even in the midst of their joy, Sahil felt the weight of what they had just committed to. The fear lingered, whispering at the edges of his mind.

After the excitement died down, Sahil retreated to his office, his heart still racing. He had made the decision, but the uncertainty remained. Picking up his phone, he dialled Aniket's number. The phone rang a few times before going to voicemail.

"Hey, Aniket," Sahil said, his voice shaky. "I just made a huge decision, and I'm freaking out a little. Call me when you can."

He hung up, his heart heavy. The breaking point had come and gone, but now, standing on the edge of the unknown, Sahil felt a strange mixture of fear and hope. They had taken the leap. Now, all that was left was to see where it led.

And as the city settled into the stillness of the night, he knew that whatever came next, they would face it together. Because sometimes, the only way to grow was to break—to shatter the old and make way for the new.

And from those broken pieces, they were ready to rise.

CHAPTER TWENTY-ONE

A Leap of Faith

Aniket stood in the middle of his now-empty office, the room eerily quiet. The once-familiar surroundings—the desk cluttered with files, the framed photos, the neatly arranged office supplies—were all gone. The walls were bare, reflecting the harsh fluorescent lights overhead. Everything about this space, which had been his second home for so many years, now felt sterile, almost hostile, as if it were reminding him that his time here was truly over.

His heart pounded in his chest as he looked around one last time. The resignation letter he had sent a few days ago had been accepted without question. The corporate world he had given so much of his life to had let him go without a second thought. He was free—free from the relentless deadlines, the soul-crushing meetings, and the ever-present weight of expectations. But that freedom came with its own burden—a terrifying uncertainty about what lay ahead.

The small cardboard box in his hands felt heavier than it should have. It was filled with the remnants of his professional life: a framed family photo, a few unread books, some personal notebooks, and a collection of pens. Everything that had once made this place feel like it belonged to him was now reduced to this box. It felt surreal. After years of dedicating himself to this career, all that was left were a few small, insignificant items.

With a deep breath, he walked toward the door, his footsteps echoing softly in the empty space. As he reached for the handle, he paused, glancing back at his desk one last time. The screen on his computer, now dark, had been his constant companion through countless long nights. The phone, once ringing off the hook with urgent calls, now sat silent. The office felt like a monument to the life he was leaving behind, a life that no longer belonged to him.

"Goodbye," he whispered under his breath, the word carrying the weight of finality. The chapter was closed. There was no going back. He had taken the leap, and now, he had to face whatever came next.

He stepped into the hallway; the building unnervingly quiet at this late hour. The familiar buzz of activity was absent, leaving only the faint hum of the air conditioning to accompany his thoughts. Each step he took felt heavy, his mind swirling with doubts. Had he made the right decision? What would come next?

When he reached the elevator, he hesitated again, his finger hovering over the button. This was it—the final moment before he left this part of his life behind. He pressed the button, and the doors slid open with a soft chime. As he stepped inside, his phone buzzed in his pocket. He pulled it out, his heart lifting slightly when he saw Sahil's name on the screen.

"Hey, Sahil," he said, his voice shaky with a mix of relief and fear. "I did it. I quit."

There was a pause before Sahil's voice came through, warm and reassuring. "Aniket, I'm proud of you. I know how hard this was."

Aniket felt his throat tighten, his eyes stinging with unshed tears. "I don't know what to do next, Sahil. I've never been without a plan before. I feel... lost."

Sahil chuckled softly on the other end. "That's okay. You don't have to have everything figured out right now. The important thing is that you took the hardest step. The rest will come."

"I've always had a plan," Aniket whispered, feeling the enormity of his decision weighing on him. "But now, I have no idea where I'm going."

"It's normal to feel scared," Sahil replied, his tone understanding. "But this is your chance to discover what you really want. You've been playing it safe for so long. Now you get to take risks, explore, and find something that truly makes you happy."

Aniket nodded, even though Sahil couldn't see him. "I guess you're right. It's just... overwhelming."

"It is," Sahil agreed. "But you've got support, Aniket. Friends, family—people who care about you. And most importantly, you've got yourself. You're stronger than you think."

A sense of calm washed over Aniket as he absorbed Sahil's words. "Thank you. I don't know what I'd do without you."

"Anytime, man," Sahil said with a smile in his voice. "And remember, if you ever feel like getting your hands dirty, the workshop is always open."

Aniket laughed softly, feeling lighter for the first time in weeks. "I might take you up on that."

They talked a bit longer, reminiscing about old times and speculating about what the future might hold. For the first time in a long while, Aniket felt a flicker of excitement, a sense that maybe, just maybe, things would be okay.

As the elevator doors slid open, he stepped out into the cool night air. The city sprawled out before him, lights twinkling in the distance, alive with possibility. He took a deep breath, feeling the crisp air fill his lungs. It was the first breath of freedom—freedom from the suffocating confines of his corporate life, from the expectations that had weighed him down for so long.

He pulled out his phone and quickly typed a message to Sahil: *Thank you. I needed this. Let's catch up soon.*

With the message sent, he smiled to himself. For the first time in years, the future felt wide open. He didn't know what was going to happen next, didn't know where this new path would lead, but he was ready to find out. He had taken the leap, and now, it was time to fly.

Meanwhile, in the small workshop on the outskirts of the city, Sahil sat at his desk, his eyes fixed on the email in front of him. The numbers and figures danced on the screen, each one more daunting than the last. The distributor deal they had secured had catapulted them into the spotlight, but it had also come with unforeseen complications. The demand for their product had exploded, and now, they were struggling to keep up.

The team had been working around the clock, doing everything they could to meet the orders, but it wasn't enough. The materials were running low, the suppliers were delayed, and the pressure was mounting. If they missed the deadlines, they could lose everything—the contract, the business, the dream they had worked so hard to build.

Sahil's phone buzzed, pulling him out of his thoughts. It was a message from Rohan: *We're out of materials again. The supplier says it'll be another two weeks.*

Sahil's heart sank. Two weeks. They didn't have that kind of time. If they couldn't meet the demand, the contract could fall through. Panic gripped him, but he forced himself to stay calm. He had been in tough situations before, but this one felt different—more urgent, more precarious.

He looked around the workshop at his team, their faces etched with exhaustion. They had been working so hard, giving everything they had. He couldn't let them down. He couldn't let this business fail.

Desperation gnawed at him as he paced the room, his mind racing for a solution. He had always been the one to take risks, to push forward even when the odds were against him. But now, with everything on the line, he felt trapped, unsure of the right move.

His phone buzzed again, this time with a message from Aniket: *Thank you. I needed this. Let's catch up soon.*

Sahil smiled, the warmth of the message cutting through his anxiety. Aniket had taken the leap, had walked away from the life that no longer served him. It reminded Sahil of his own journey—of the risks he had taken, the faith he had placed in himself and his team.

Taking a deep breath, Sahil knew what he had to do. He picked up the phone and dialled the number of a local supplier he had been hesitant to contact. Their terms were steep, and the risks were high, but it was the only way forward.

The phone rang twice before a voice answered. "Hello?"

"Hi, this is Sahil Sharma. I'm calling about a potential order..."

The negotiation was tense, and the stakes were high, but by the time Sahil hung up, his heart was pounding with a mix of fear and hope. He had secured the materials, though at a cost. The pressure was still immense, but they had a chance—a chance to make it work.

Turning to his team, Sahil's voice was steady as he spoke. "We've got a new supplier. It's going to be tough, but we're going to make it work. I believe in us. We've come too far to give up now."

A cheer went up around the room, the energy shifting as the team returned to work with renewed determination. Sahil watched them for a moment, his heart swelling with pride. They weren't just colleagues—they were a family. And together, they would face whatever challenges lay ahead.

He picked up his phone and sent a quick message to Aniket: *Took a leap of faith today. Scary, but worth it. Catch up soon.*

As he slipped the phone into his pocket, a smile tugged at his lips. The road ahead was uncertain, filled with risks and obstacles, but for the first time in a long while, he felt confident that they were on the right path.

Sometimes, the only way forward is to take a leap of faith, to trust that even if you don't see the ground beneath you, it will be there when you land.

And as the workshop buzzed with activity, filled with the sound of hope and determination, Sahil knew that they were ready to rise.

CHAPTER TWENTY-TWO

Starting Anew

Aniket sat at his small kitchen table, staring blankly at the notebook in front of him. The morning sunlight filtered through the window, casting a gentle glow over the room, but it did little to ease the tightness in his chest. He tapped his pen absentmindedly against the blank page, frustration mounting with every passing minute. For two weeks, this had been his routine—sitting, thinking, trying to find direction—and yet nothing came.

It had been two weeks since he left his corporate job, two weeks since he had finally taken that leap of faith. And yet, instead of feeling liberated, instead of embracing the freedom he thought quitting would bring, he felt adrift. Without the structure of his old life, the steady rhythm of work, meetings, and deadlines, he was lost. The blank pages in front of him mirrored the uncertainty inside, the fear that gnawed at him day and night.

He sighed, running a hand through his dishevelled hair. He had thought that walking away from his old life would open a world of possibilities. But now, faced with the vast emptiness of unplanned days, it felt more like a void than an opportunity. The ideas he once cherished seemed to have evaporated, and the dreams he had hoped would guide him felt distant and irrelevant.

His phone buzzed on the table, shaking him from his thoughts. He glanced at the screen: Sahil.

"How's it going, man? Want to grab lunch today?"

Aniket stared at the message, his fingers hovering over the keys. The thought of facing Sahil, of having to explain why he was still stuck in the same mental space, filled him with dread. But he knew he couldn't keep avoiding his friend forever. Maybe getting out would help him clear his head, at least for a little while.

"Sure," he typed. "Where do you want to meet?"

Sahil replied almost instantly. "That café on Maple Street? 1 p.m.?"

Aniket confirmed the plan, then set his phone down, staring again at the blank page in front of him. A deep sigh escaped him as he stood up, running his hand across his face. The small apartment felt like a cage—a constant reminder of the uncertainty that now defined his days. He wandered to the mirror in the hallway, catching sight of his reflection. Dark circles framed his tired eyes, his hair stuck up in uneven tufts. He looked as worn out as he felt.

"Get it together," he muttered to himself.

Grabbing his jacket and keys, he stepped outside into the cool air. The bustling city streets were a welcome distraction, the sounds of traffic and chatter offering a sense of normalcy. He walked slowly, taking in the sights of people moving purposefully, everyone with a destination, while he had none. It was both comforting and disheartening—life moving forward, while he remained stuck.

By the time he reached the café, Sahil was already seated near the window, waving him over with a broad smile. "Hey, Aniket! Good to see you!"

Aniket forced a smile as he sat down. "Good to see you too."

They ordered coffee, and for a while, the conversation was light—workshop updates from Sahil, small talk about the weather, and anecdotes from old times. But the weight of unspoken questions hung in the air, and soon enough, Sahil's voice softened as he leaned forward.

"So... how's it going? Adjusting to the new life?"

Aniket stared into his coffee, tracing the rim of his cup with his finger. "It's... harder than I thought," he admitted. "I thought quitting would bring clarity, that I'd finally know what I really want. But instead, I feel lost."

Sahil nodded, his eyes filled with understanding. "It's completely normal to feel that way. You've spent so long working toward one thing, and now everything's changed. It's going to take time."

Aniket shook his head, frustration bubbling up inside him. "I just thought I'd have more direction. That something would click, you know? But right now, I feel like I'm just... drifting."

Sahil reached across the table, resting a hand on Aniket's arm. "It's okay not to have everything figured out right away. This is your time to explore, to figure out what makes you happy. There's no rush."

"But I don't even know where to start," Aniket murmured, his throat tightening. "I've always had a plan, always known what was next. Now, there's nothing."

Sahil smiled gently. "Start with what you love. What's something that makes you feel alive? Something that makes the world fade away?"

Aniket frowned, his mind drawing a blank. It had been so long since he had done something for the sheer joy of it. For years, he had been chasing goals that, in retrospect, seemed hollow. He had forgotten what it felt like to pursue something out of passion rather than obligation.

"I don't even know anymore," he said softly.

Sahil's eyes softened. "Then that's your first step—finding what you love again. Try new things, take risks, see where it leads. There's no pressure to get it right the first time."

Aniket looked up, meeting Sahil's gaze. "What if I don't find it? What if there's nothing out there for me?"

Sahil squeezed his arm, his voice steady. "You're not empty, Aniket. You're just searching. And you will find it. I believe in you."

Aniket's chest tightened with gratitude, but doubt still clung to him like a weight. "I just wish I knew where to go from here."

Sahil leaned back, his smile unwavering. "Life isn't about having all the answers, Aniket. It's about learning as you go. Every wrong turn teaches you something valuable. And besides, you've taken risks before—bigger risks than you realize."

Aniket thought back to his decision to leave the corporate world, the countless hours spent agonizing over whether it was the right choice. He had taken the leap, but now it felt like he was floundering, waiting for something to catch him.

"What if I fail again?" he whispered.

Sahil's eyes twinkled. "Then you get back up and try again. That's how we grow. You've already proven that you can take risks. This is just the next step."

Aniket let out a shaky breath, a small smile tugging at the corners of his lips. "I don't know how you always manage to sound so sure."

"It's not about being sure," Sahil replied, his tone gentle. "It's about trusting yourself enough to keep going, even when you're unsure. You've got time, Aniket. There's no deadline. Life is long, and it's full of second chances."

Aniket nodded, feeling a flicker of hope for the first time in weeks. He didn't have all the answers, but maybe that was okay. Maybe, as Sahil said, the first step was simply letting go of the need for control and allowing himself to explore.

"I'll try," he said quietly, meeting Sahil's gaze with a hint of determination. "I'll take that first step."

Sahil grinned, lifting his coffee cup in a toast. "To the first step, and all the ones that follow."

Aniket clinked his cup against Sahil's, the warmth of possibility blooming in his chest. He didn't know where this path would lead, but for the first time in weeks, he felt ready to start walking.

Later that evening, Sahil stood in his workshop, the hum of machinery filling the air as his team gathered around the latest prototype. The sleek motor gleamed under the overhead lights, a testament to their hard work and ingenuity.

"We've come a long way," Sahil began, his voice steady but filled with excitement. "This motor is more efficient and powerful than anything we've built before. It's the future of our business."

His team nodded, eyes wide with anticipation. They had worked tirelessly to reach this moment, pushing through setbacks and obstacles that might have stopped others. Now, they had something tangible, something that could truly set them apart.

"But," Sahil continued, his tone more serious, "there's still a lot of risk involved. We need more time, more resources, and there's no guarantee it'll work out. But I believe in this. I believe in all of you."

The team exchanged glances; their faces resolute. "We're in this together," Rohan said, his voice firm. "Whatever it takes."

Priya nodded, her eyes bright with determination. "We've come this far. We're not backing down now."

Sahil felt a swell of pride as he looked around at his team. They had faced so much adversity, yet here they stood, ready to push forward again. He knew the road ahead would be tough, but he also knew they had what it took to succeed.

"Thank you," Sahil said, his voice thick with emotion. "We're going to make this work."

They worked late into the night, the hum of machinery and the soft murmur of voices filling the workshop. And as the first light of dawn filtered through the windows, casting a soft glow over the room, Sahil knew that they were on the brink of something extraordinary.

Because sometimes, the only way to build something new was to let go of the past, to take a leap of faith, and trust that the future would unfold as it was meant to. And standing there, surrounded by his team, Sahil knew that they were exactly where they were meant to be.

CHAPTER TWENTY-THREE

The Power of Persistence

Aniket sat on the edge of his bed, his eyes focused on the floor, his mind clouded with uncertainty. The pale morning light filtered through the curtains, casting long shadows across the room, but it did little to ease the weight pressing down on him. The excitement he had once felt after quitting his job had faded into the background, leaving behind only doubt and a growing sense of fear. Each day felt longer than the last, a relentless loop of unspoken questions and unresolved uncertainties.

He glanced at his phone lying idle on the nightstand. No new messages. The initial wave of support from his former colleagues had dried up, replaced by a silence that made him feel even more disconnected. He had expected more from this new chapter in his life, but instead, it felt like he was standing at a crossroads, unsure which path to take.

In a moment of hesitation, Aniket opened his laptop. He found himself staring at the familiar company logo of his old workplace, the careers page in front of him offering the very thing he had walked away from: stability. His fingers hovered over the keyboard as he scrolled through the open positions. It was tempting. After all, he had spent years climbing that corporate ladder, sacrificing his time and energy in pursuit of success. Could he really go back now? Would it be so bad to admit defeat?

His chest tightened at the thought of returning to that life. He had left for a reason—a reason that seemed to blur the longer he stared at the screen. Aniket slammed the laptop shut, frustration bubbling up inside him. Every path felt wrong, and the pressure to find the "right" one was suffocating.

He stood and walked over to the window, resting his forehead against the cool glass as he gazed out at the city below. The world outside moved forward, busy and chaotic, yet he felt paralyzed, stuck in a cycle of indecision. He had been part of that world once, thriving in its fast pace. But now? Now he felt like an outsider, watching from the sidelines.

The buzzing of his phone pulled him from his thoughts. He looked down, his heart lifting slightly when he saw Sahil's name.

"Hey, Aniket," Sahil's voice came through, steady and warm. "I've been thinking about you. How are you holding up?"

Aniket swallowed hard, trying to keep the rising emotions at bay. "I don't know, Sahil. I feel like I've made a mistake."

There was a pause on the other end. "What do you mean?"

Aniket sighed, running a hand through his dishevelled hair. "I thought quitting would bring me clarity, you know? That it would help me figure out what I really want. But now, I just feel lost. I've been thinking about going back. I've even been looking at job postings."

Sahil's voice softened. "It's okay to feel like that, Aniket. You've gone through a huge change. It's natural to have doubts."

"But what if I made the wrong decision?" Aniket's voice trembled. "What if I'm not cut out for this? I feel like I'm wasting time, and I'm not getting anywhere."

"You're not wasting time," Sahil replied firmly. "You're giving yourself space to figure things out. And that takes time. It's not a failure to be uncertain."

Aniket closed his eyes, the weight of his own expectations pressing down on him. "It just feels like I'm not doing anything. Like I'm stuck."

Sahil let out a gentle sigh. "You're not failing, Aniket. You're doing something most people don't even attempt—you're trying to find your path. You're brave for that alone."

"What if I never figure it out?" Aniket's voice was barely above a whisper. "What if I never find what I'm looking for?"

Sahil's response was filled with quiet strength. "Then you keep trying. You take it one step at a time. The important thing is not giving up."

Aniket felt a tear slip down his cheek, the vulnerability of the moment catching him off guard. "I don't know if I have the strength for that."

"You do," Sahil said, his voice steady. "You've got more strength than you realize, Aniket. And whatever happens, I'm here for you. You don't have to go through this alone."

Aniket's chest tightened with gratitude, the weight of his doubts easing just slightly. "Thank you, Sahil. I needed that."

"Anytime," Sahil replied warmly. "Listen, why don't you come by the workshop? I've got something to show you."

Aniket hesitated, uncertainty still swirling in his mind. But he knew he needed to get out of his own head, to step away from the spiral of doubt. "Okay," he said finally, his voice steadier. "I'll be there."

The workshop was alive with the sounds of industry as Aniket stepped inside—machinery humming, the smell of fresh paint and metal in the air. The energy in the room was palpable, a stark contrast to the stillness he had been drowning in at home. It felt good to be surrounded by people with purpose, people moving forward with a shared vision.

Sahil spotted him and waved, making his way over with a broad smile. "Aniket! I'm glad you came."

Aniket smiled back, though it still felt forced. "Thanks for inviting me."

"I wanted to show you something." Sahil gestured for Aniket to follow him toward the back of the workshop, where a group of engineers stood around a machine.

The machine gleamed under the lights, sleek and modern. There was a buzz of excitement among the team as they tinkered with the final adjustments.

"This," Sahil said, pride evident in his voice, "is our newest model. The most advanced piece of equipment we've ever designed. We've been working on it for months, and it's finally ready."

Aniket looked at the machine, awe and a tinge of envy rising within him. It was a symbol of everything he felt he was missing—a project with purpose, something tangible. He glanced at Sahil's team, their faces filled with pride and accomplishment. It was clear they were united by a shared goal.

"That's incredible," Aniket said quietly. "You've really done something amazing."

Sahil's smile softened. "It wasn't easy, Aniket. There were setbacks. A lot of them. But we kept pushing. We didn't give up. And now, we're seeing the results."

Aniket looked down, feeling the familiar weight of self-doubt settling over him. "I'm not sure I have the persistence for something like this. I feel so... lost."

Sahil placed a hand on his shoulder, his gaze understanding. "You're not lost. You're searching. And there's a big difference."

"But what if I never find it?" Aniket's voice cracked with emotion. "What if I never figure out what I'm supposed to do?"

Sahil squeezed his shoulder, his voice steady. "Then you keep trying. You don't quit just because it's hard. Persistence is about moving forward, even when it feels like you're not getting anywhere."

Aniket felt a flicker of hope, though the doubt still lingered. "What if I don't have the strength?"

"You do, Aniket," Sahil said firmly. "You've already taken the hardest step—you left behind what wasn't working. Now you just need to trust yourself enough to find what will."

Aniket nodded, his gratitude overwhelming. "Thanks, Sahil. I don't know what I'd do without your support."

Sahil smiled, his eyes warm. "We're in this together. You're not alone."

Over the following weeks, the atmosphere in the workshop grew more intense as the launch of their new product neared. The stakes were high, but so was the sense of excitement. Aniket spent more time at the workshop, watching Sahil and his team, absorbing the energy of their persistence and hard work. It was contagious, this relentless pursuit of a goal, and for the first time in a while, Aniket began to feel that spark of hope reigniting within himself.

Finally, the day of the launch arrived. The workshop was filled with investors, clients, and media, all eager to see the new product that Sahil and his team had poured their hearts into. Aniket stood at the back, watching as Sahil took the stage to address the crowd.

"This is the result of years of hard work, countless hours, and a belief in something bigger than ourselves," Sahil said, his voice steady. "This machine represents our future, a future we built because we refused to give up, even when things got tough."

He unveiled the machine, and the crowd murmured in admiration as the polished equipment shone under the lights. The demonstration went off without a hitch, the machine working flawlessly. Applause erupted from the audience, and Sahil's team erupted in smiles and high fives. It was a moment of triumph.

Aniket felt a hand on his shoulder and turned to see Sahil standing beside him, eyes shining with pride. "We did it, Aniket."

Aniket nodded, his own emotions welling up. "You did it, Sahil. You never gave up."

Sahil smiled softly. "Neither did you. Don't forget that."

Aniket looked out at the bustling room, the sense of accomplishment hanging heavy in the air. The power of persistence was not just about pushing through challenges. It was about trusting that every step, even the uncertain ones, was leading somewhere important. And as he stood there, surrounded by people who had built something extraordinary through sheer will and belief, Aniket realized that maybe he was on the right path after all.

Maybe, just maybe, he was starting to understand the power of persistence himself.

And as the evening wore on, Aniket felt lighter than he had in weeks. He knew there would still be moments of doubt, still days when the road ahead seemed unclear. But he also knew that, like Sahil, he had the strength to keep going. To persist.

Because the only way to find what you're looking for is to keep searching, to keep moving forward, no matter how hard it gets.

CHAPTER TWENTY-FOUR

The Hollow Success

Aniket walked into the sleek, glass-walled office building, his footsteps echoing against the polished marble floor. The reflection in the mirrored walls revealed a man who appeared composed and confident, but his eyes betrayed a weariness and a quiet doubt that simmered beneath the surface. He had landed the job—a respectable mid-level management position in a well-known firm, one with a salary and benefits that would silence those nagging questions about his career choices. On paper, it seemed like a victory, a step back into the world he had once thrived in. But as the elevator ascended to the twenty-fourth floor, he felt a growing unease, an emptiness that gnawed at him.

The elevator doors slid open, revealing a bustling open-floor office space. Rows of cubicles lined the area, with glass-walled conference rooms on one side. The click of keyboards, low murmurs of conversation, and the occasional ring of a phone filled the air. It was a familiar soundscape, one that should have comforted him, but instead, it felt foreign, almost as though he were stepping back into a life that no longer belonged to him.

"Aniket!" A bright voice broke through his thoughts, and he turned to see a tall, professional-looking woman approaching with an outstretched hand and a warm smile. "Welcome aboard! I'm Priya, your onboarding coordinator. So glad to finally meet you in person."

Aniket mustered a polite smile, shaking her hand. "Thank you, Priya. It's nice to be here."

She led him through the office, giving him the standard tour—introducing him to the different departments, pointing out the break room, the conference rooms, and eventually showing him to his own workspace. It was a corner cubicle with a large window that offered a sweeping view of the city. "Here's your desk. Everything's set up for you. If you need anything, don't hesitate to let me know," she said cheerfully.

Aniket nodded, his gaze shifting to the view outside. The city stretched out below him, full of life and movement, yet he felt completely disconnected from it. It was as though the vibrant world beyond the window was part of someone else's story. "Thank you, Priya. I appreciate it."

She smiled, seemingly sensing his hesitation. "Take your time getting settled in. The first day can be a lot, but I'm sure you'll do great."

As she walked away, Aniket sat down at his desk, placing his hands on the cool surface. The computer screen flickered to life, the company logo glowing softly in the corner. Everything about this space was pristine—too pristine, like a well-orchestrated set in a play he hadn't rehearsed for. He had secured the job, the title, the status. Yet, instead of feeling accomplished, a hollow ache settled in his chest.

The day passed in a blur of handshakes, introductions, and orientation meetings. His new colleagues greeted him with courteous smiles, and they exchanged the usual pleasantries, but Aniket couldn't shake the feeling of detachment. He moved through the motions, answered questions, and listened to presentations, all the while feeling as though he were watching himself from a distance. By the time the day came to an end, his head throbbed from the sheer volume of information, and his heart felt heavier than ever.

As the elevator descended, Aniket stared blankly at the floor. The soft hum of the machinery was the only sound in the otherwise silent space. When the doors opened, he stepped out into the cool evening air, the city's usual hustle and bustle swirling around him. The streets were alive with the sounds of traffic, footsteps, and distant chatter, but none of it seemed to penetrate the fog of disconnection that surrounded him. He made his way to his car, feeling like a stranger in a place that once felt so familiar.

The drive home was quiet, the radio turned off as his thoughts consumed him. When he finally stepped into his apartment, the silence was deafening. He dropped his bag by the door and sank onto the couch, his head in his hands. The same question kept echoing in his mind: *Is this what success feels like?*

He had thought that getting another job would bring back the sense of purpose he had lost, but instead, it had only deepened the void. It felt like he had traded one empty title for another, one set of chains for a new pair. The sense of accomplishment he had expected was nowhere to be found. All that remained was a hollow sense of going through the motions, as though his life was on autopilot.

His phone buzzed on the table, and he picked it up to see Sahil's name. For a moment, he hesitated, unsure if he wanted to share the turmoil that had been brewing inside him. But then, with a deep breath, he answered the call.

"Hey, Aniket!" Sahil's voice was filled with warmth, and Aniket felt a brief surge of comfort. "How was the first day at the new job?"

Aniket closed his eyes, fighting the lump that was forming in his throat. "It was... fine," he said, his voice strained. "Everyone was nice, and the office is great, but... I don't know, Sahil. It doesn't feel right."

Sahil's tone softened, concern creeping into his words. "What do you mean? You were excited about this opportunity."

Aniket leaned back on the couch, staring up at the ceiling. "I thought getting this job would make everything better—that it would put me back on track. But all I feel is... empty. It's like I'm just going through the motions, and none of it really matters."

There was a pause, and when Sahil spoke again, his voice was gentle. "It's okay to feel that way, Aniket. You're still adjusting. It takes time to settle into a new routine."

"But what if this isn't what I want?" Aniket's voice cracked, his frustration spilling over. "What if I'm just fooling myself into thinking this is the answer when it's not? I feel like I'm trying to fit into a life that doesn't fit anymore."

Sahil remained quiet for a moment, then replied with quiet conviction. "Then maybe it's time to stop trying to fit into that life. Maybe it's time to figure out what you actually want—what makes you feel alive. You've been searching for so long, Aniket, and that's okay. It's okay to take a step back and rethink what really matters to you."

Tears stung at Aniket's eyes, the weight of his own doubts pressing down on him. "I just don't know where to start," he admitted, his voice barely above a whisper. "I feel so lost."

"You're not lost," Sahil said firmly. "You're finding your way. And that takes time. Start with what makes you happy—what gives you even a small spark of joy. You've got the strength to figure this out, Aniket. You always have."

A lump rose in Aniket's throat, his heart aching with gratitude. "Thank you, Sahil. I needed to hear that."

"Anytime," Sahil replied warmly. "And listen, the workshop is always open if you ever want to get away from the corporate world for a bit. You know you're welcome here."

Aniket smiled for what felt like the first time in days—a small, genuine smile. "I might just take you up on that."

After they hung up, Aniket sat in the quiet of his apartment, his heart a little lighter but still weighed down by uncertainty. He didn't have all the answers, but something Sahil had said stuck with him: *It's okay to take a step back.* Maybe that was what he needed most—not another title, not another job, but time. Time to reflect, time to figure out what truly mattered.

At the workshop, Sahil sat at his desk, reviewing the latest financial reports. The numbers looked good—better than they had expected. The success of their latest product launch had exceeded their projections, and orders were coming in faster than they could fulfil. It was a triumph, a moment they had worked toward for months.

And yet, for Sahil, the satisfaction went beyond the numbers. It wasn't about the money or the recognition. It was about the journey—about the risks they had taken, the challenges they had overcome, and the passion that had driven them forward, even in the face of uncertainty. He glanced out of his office window at the workshop floor below. His team moved with purpose, their faces filled with pride as they assembled the next batch of machines.

He picked up his phone and scrolled through the photos he had taken over the past few months—the team celebrating the first successful test run, the late nights filled with laughter and camaraderie, the moments of doubt that had given way to quiet victories. Each image was a reminder of how far they had come and how much they had built together.

Sahil stood up, feeling a surge of gratitude as he walked down to the workshop floor. His team greeted him with smiles, their warmth and support palpable.

"How's it going, boss?" Rohan called out, wiping the grease from his hands.

Sahil grinned, feeling a deep sense of contentment. "Going great, thanks to all of you."

Priya nodded, her eyes bright with pride. "We couldn't have done it without you, Sahil. You believed in us, even when things got tough."

Sahil shook his head, his smile softening. "We did this together. Every single one of us."

The night stretched on, the hum of machinery and the sound of laughter filling the space. There were still challenges ahead, but Sahil knew they were ready. They had proven that persistence, belief, and teamwork could carry them through even the most difficult times.

And as Sahil looked around at his team—his family—he knew that this was where he was meant to be. This was his success—not the hollow kind built on titles and prestige, but the kind built on passion, purpose, and people who believed in each other.

And as Aniket sat alone in his apartment, contemplating the life he was trying to build, he realized that he had a long way to go. But he wasn't alone. He had friends, family, and the quiet strength to keep moving forward.

Because sometimes, success wasn't about the destination—it was about the journey, and the courage to keep going.

CHAPTER TWENTY-FIVE

The Awakening

Aniket sat on the edge of his bed, the early morning light casting a soft glow over the room, illuminating the chaos that surrounded him. A half-empty coffee cup sat on the nightstand, long forgotten. Crumpled papers were scattered across the floor, and his laptop, left open but untouched for hours, silently testified to his restless, sleepless night. His eyes were heavy, dark circles betraying the weight of exhaustion, but it was not only physical fatigue—his thoughts were tangled in a web of regrets, fears, and unspoken doubts that refused to untangle.

He glanced at his phone. It was barely past 6 a.m., but sleep had eluded him once again. The familiar ache in his chest had grown more persistent with each passing day—a hollow emptiness that gnawed at his insides. The weeks since starting his new job had passed in a blur, and the initial excitement that had accompanied the fresh start had long since dissolved, replaced by the monotony of routine and a deepening sense of discontent.

A sobering realization had started to dawn on him, one that terrified him more than any uncertain future ever could. He wasn't running toward something; he was running away. Away from the spectre of failure, from the crushing expectations of himself and others. And in his frantic escape, he had lost sight of who he was, of what truly mattered, of what could ignite that fire of purpose within him.

Closing his eyes, he tried to steady his breathing. His entire life had been built on carefully calculated moves—each step measured to avoid failure, to stay within the safe confines of success and expectations. But now, sitting here in the silence of dawn, he felt the walls of those boundaries closing in on him, suffocating him with each passing second.

His phone buzzed suddenly, cutting through his thoughts like a sharp blade. He picked it up, and his stomach tightened when he saw the notification: an email from his boss. His eyes skimmed the message, but the words blurred in a haze of mounting anxiety.

We need to discuss your performance in the upcoming meeting. There have been some concerns...

Setting the phone down, Aniket's hands trembled. The meeting. He had been dreading it for days, the sense of impending doom hanging over him like a storm cloud. He knew his performance had been lacklustre, distracted. But the thought of being called out, of facing his shortcomings head-on, made his chest tighten and his pulse race with dread.

Pushing himself to his feet, his legs felt shaky as he crossed the room and stood at the window. Outside, the city was slowly waking up—cars trickled down the streets, and the distant murmur of life started to grow louder. But Aniket felt cut off from it all, isolated and adrift in a world that no longer made sense to him.

He pressed his forehead against the cool glass of the window, watching as his breath fogged up the view. He didn't want to go to that meeting, didn't want to face the disappointment that he knew was waiting for him. More than that, he didn't want to keep living like this—driven by fear, by the constant need to prove something to himself and the world.

His phone buzzed again. This time, the notification lifted his heart ever so slightly. It was a message from Sahil:

Hey, Aniket. I've been thinking about you. I know things have been tough lately, but you're not alone. You've got this, whatever happens.

A lump formed in Aniket's throat as he read the words, his eyes stinging. He typed back a quick reply, his hands still trembling.

Thank you, Sahil. I needed that. I'm just... struggling. I don't know what to do.

Sahil's response came almost immediately:

Take it one step at a time. Don't be so hard on yourself. You're stronger than you think. And remember, it's okay to fail. It's part of the process.

Aniket stared at the words, his chest tightening as the message sank in. *It's okay to fail.* The notion felt foreign, even absurd. He had spent his entire life avoiding failure, carefully constructing his choices to minimize risk, to keep himself within the safety of success. But here he was, staring failure in the face, wondering if maybe, just maybe, Sahil was right.

Taking a deep breath, Aniket's mind churned with uncertainty. He didn't have all the answers. He didn't know what the future held. But he knew one thing: he couldn't continue down this path, imprisoned by fear.

He picked up his phone again, his fingers hovering over the screen before he dialled his boss's number. His heart thudded in his chest as the phone rang, but when his boss answered, Aniket spoke with a clarity and calm that surprised even himself.

"I'd like to cancel the meeting," Aniket said, the decision firm in his voice. "I think it's time for me to take a step back and reevaluate what I want from my career."

There was a pause on the other end of the line. When his boss spoke again, the voice was surprised but not unkind. "Are you sure, Aniket? We can work through this. Address the concerns."

"I appreciate that," Aniket replied, "but I think this is something I need to figure out on my own. I need some time to reflect and decide where I want to go from here."

The conversation was brief, and his resignation was met with reluctant understanding. When Aniket hung up, he felt a wave of relief wash over him—a lightness he hadn't felt in months. He had taken the first step toward something new, something unknown, and it felt liberating.

The room around him was still a mess—books piled high on the desk, half-finished notes scattered across the floor, ideas scrawled in a frenzy on the whiteboard but never pursued. All of it mirrored the inner chaos he had been living with. But as he looked at the mess now, it didn't feel overwhelming. It felt like a place to begin.

He walked over to the whiteboard and wiped it clean with a swipe of his hand. Then, with steady fingers, he picked up a marker and wrote a single word in bold, black letters:

Fear.

He stepped back and stared at the word. It felt simple, almost too simple, but it carried the weight of everything he had been grappling with—every decision, every hesitation, every sleepless night. He had let fear drive his life for too long.

Setting down the marker, he grabbed it again and wrote another word beneath it:

Courage.

He stood there for a moment, the two words staring back at him like a challenge. This was what he had been searching for—not just a way out of fear, but the courage to embrace it, to accept that it was part of the journey. It wasn't about avoiding failure anymore; it was about learning to take risks, to stumble, to rise again.

He felt calmer now, more centered. The fear was still there, lurking in the corners of his mind, but it no longer felt like a prison. It felt like a choice—one he could face, one he could overcome.

Aniket picked up his phone once more, his hands steady as he typed a message to Sahil:

Thank you for everything. I think I'm finally ready to figure things out.

He hit send, a small smile tugging at the corners of his lips as he put the phone down. He didn't know what the future would bring, but for the first time in a long time, that uncertainty didn't paralyze him. It filled him with hope.

Walking over to the window, he watched as the city came to life below him. It was the same view as always, but today it felt different—like the world was opening, full of possibility. He took a deep breath, his heart light with the knowledge that he was finally ready to step into that world and see where the path would lead.

Meanwhile, in a small workshop on the outskirts of the city, Sahil stood at his workbench, a familiar sense of anticipation buzzing through his veins. The past few weeks had been a whirlwind of activity, orders pouring in faster than his team could fill them. But today felt different. Today, there was something more in the air—a feeling that something significant was on the horizon.

Rohan hurried over; his face flushed with excitement. "Sahil, it's ready. The prototype is complete."

Sahil felt his heart skip a beat, a mixture of pride and nerves rising in his chest. This project had been months in the making—an ambitious design that had pushed their skills and creativity to the limit. But now, standing on the edge of something big, Sahil knew it was all about to come together.

"Show me," he said, his voice steady, though his pulse raced.

They moved to the center of the workshop, where the prototype sat under the bright lights. It gleamed, sleek and polished, a testament to the team's innovation and relentless hard work. Sahil approached it slowly, his heart swelling with pride as he ran his fingers over the cool metal surface.

"We did it," he whispered, awe in his voice. "We actually did it."

The team gathered around, holding their breath as Sahil flipped the switch. The machine hummed to life, performing its programmed tasks with flawless precision. There was a moment of silence before the room erupted in cheers, the sound of triumph filling the air.

Sahil looked around at the faces of his team—the people who had believed in this vision, who had worked tirelessly to make it a reality. They had overcome every obstacle, every setback, and now, standing here, they were finally witnessing the fruits of their labour.

"This is just the beginning," Rohan said, clapping Sahil on the back. "We're about to change everything."

Sahil smiled, his heart full. They had come so far, and the journey had been anything but easy. But it had been worth every challenge, every late night. This was success—not just in the business sense, but in the sense of creating something meaningful, something lasting.

As the celebration continued, Sahil stepped outside to catch his breath. The cool night air felt refreshing against his skin as he looked up at the stars, feeling a deep sense of peace. This was what it meant to follow your passion, to create something from nothing. The satisfaction went beyond financial gain or recognition—it was about the journey, the people you shared it with, and the courage to keep moving forward.

His phone buzzed in his pocket, and he smiled when he saw Aniket's message.

Thank you for everything. I think I'm finally ready to figure things out.

Sahil quickly typed a reply:

I knew you would be. I'm proud of you, Aniket. Whatever you decide, I'm here for you.

As he slipped the phone back into his pocket, Sahil knew that they were both on their way. Aniket had begun his journey, and Sahil was ready for the next chapter in his own.

Because sometimes, the greatest breakthroughs don't come from the mind—they come from the heart. And Sahil was ready to follow his, wherever it led.

The Entrepreneurial Spirit

Aniket sat at the small, cluttered desk in his living room, his heart racing between excitement and fear. The late afternoon sun bathed the room in a warm, golden glow, illuminating scattered papers, an open laptop, and a stack of freshly printed business cards. The bold letters on the cards felt both real and daunting: **"Aniket Sharma: Independent Consultant."**

He picked up one of the cards, running his fingers over the raised letters. This was it—the first step of a new journey. He had spent weeks preparing meticulously, diving deep into research, refining his ideas, and planning every detail of his consultancy. From books to seminars, late-night calls with Sahil, and endless hours of planning, he had absorbed every piece of advice he could.

Yet, sitting here in the quiet of his apartment, the reality hit him harder than he expected. The thought of starting from scratch, of building something entirely his own, felt both exhilarating and terrifying. There were no guarantees, no steady pay checks, just him and the belief that he could carve out a meaningful path.

He set the business card down, his fingers trembling. He had left behind the security of a structured career, but the uncertainty ahead cast long shadows. He was standing on the precipice of the unknown, his fear a constant whisper in the back of his mind, telling him all the ways this could go wrong.

His phone buzzed, breaking the silence. Seeing Sahil's name on the screen, Aniket's heart lifted just a little.

"Hey, Sahil," Aniket said, trying to keep his voice steady. "What's up?"

"Aniket! Just thinking about you," came Sahil's warm, infectious tone. "How's the new venture coming along?"

Aniket leaned back, a smile tugging at his lips despite the tightness in his chest. "It's... coming along. Website's live, I've reached out to a few potential clients, and everything's in place. But honestly, Sahil, I'm terrified."

Sahil laughed, a sound that always had a way of easing Aniket's nerves. "Good! That means you're on the right track. If it wasn't scary, it wouldn't be worth it."

Aniket exhaled, the weight on his shoulders easing just a bit. "I know you're right. But I can't stop thinking about everything that could go wrong, all the ways I could fail."

Sahil's voice softened, carrying an empathy that calmed Aniket. "That's normal, my friend. Failure is part of the process—it's how you learn, grow, and get better. You've already done the hardest part by starting. Now, it's about persistence and believing in what you're building."

Aniket closed his eyes, letting Sahil's words sink in. "I've always been afraid of failing, but I can't let that fear control me anymore."

"You're stronger than you know, Aniket. You have so much to offer, and there are people out there who need exactly what you bring. Take it one step at a time. You've got this."

A wave of gratitude washed over Aniket, his heart lightening. "Thank you, Sahil. I really needed that."

"Anytime," Sahil said, the warmth in his voice making Aniket smile. "And remember, you're not alone. If you ever need help, you know where to find me."

They talked for a little while longer, reminiscing about their school days and swapping stories about their future. For the first time in weeks, Aniket felt a calm settle over him—a quiet confidence that maybe, just maybe, he was on the right path.

After they hung up, Aniket glanced again at the stack of business cards. This was his chance to make a difference, to take control of his future. His heart beat a little steadier now, as a renewed resolve surged through him. Picking up his phone, he scrolled to the number of one of the potential clients he had been hesitant to contact. He took a deep breath and dialled.

The phone rang once, twice, before a voice answered. "Hello?"

Aniket's heart raced. "Hi, this is Aniket Sharma. I'm an independent consultant, and I was hoping to set up a meeting to discuss how I might be able to help with your current project."

There was a pause, and Aniket held his breath. Finally, the voice on the other end spoke. "That sounds great, Aniket. Let's schedule something for next week."

Relief and a burst of pride flooded him. "Thank you. I'll wait for your availability and we can finalize the details."

They wrapped up the call, and as Aniket set the phone down, he smiled to himself. He had taken the first step, faced his fear, and it had paid off. There would be more challenges ahead, of that, he was sure. But for the first time, Aniket felt like he was moving in the right direction.

Meanwhile, in the bustling workshop that had become the nerve center of his expanding business, Sahil stood at the head of the conference table, his heart pounding with excitement. The past few months had been a whirlwind—the success of their product launch had thrust them into the national spotlight.

Sahil looked around the room at the faces of his team—the people who had been with him through every setback, every late night. They had built this together, and now, they were on the cusp of something even bigger.

"We've just received the official confirmation," Sahil announced, his voice steady, but his eyes gleaming. "We've been invited to present at the National Innovation Summit next month."

The room fell silent for a moment, the magnitude of his words sinking in. Then, cheers erupted, filling the room with a sense of victory. His team leaped to their feet, clapping, cheering, celebrating. Sahil smiled, watching them with a mix of pride and humility. This was what it meant to follow a dream, to build something from the ground up. They had faced so many challenges, but now, standing on the brink of even greater success, Sahil knew it had all been worth it.

"This is just the beginning," Sahil said once the room quieted down. "We've worked hard to get here, and now, we have the chance to show the world what we're capable of. But we won't stop here. We'll keep innovating, keep pushing ourselves to new heights."

After the meeting, Sahil stepped outside, the cool night air wrapping around him. The city lights twinkled in the distance as he thought of Aniket and their earlier conversation. Sahil felt a surge of pride for his friend. Aniket had taken a brave step, leaving behind security to follow his own path. It wouldn't be easy, but Sahil knew that Aniket had the resilience and strength to succeed.

He pulled out his phone and typed a quick message to Aniket.

Remember, it's not about the destination. It's about the journey. Keep going, one step at a time. You've got this.

Sahil smiled as he hit send. He knew there would be hurdles ahead for both, but that was part of the adventure.

In his small apartment, Aniket sat at his desk, staring at the blank page in front of him. His heart was lighter now, filled with determination and a quiet resolve. He didn't know what lay ahead or if his consultancy would succeed, but he knew he was ready to try.

He picked up his pen and wrote the first line of his business plan, the words flowing naturally. He was building something real, something meaningful. And no matter what challenges came his way, he was ready.

Because the entrepreneurial spirit wasn't about success or failure—it was about the courage to dream, to take risks, and to create something from nothing. It was about the journey, the lessons learned, and the people who helped you along the way.

As the night deepened, Aniket knew that he was prepared for whatever came next. He glanced at the business cards once more, the name of his new venture standing out boldly: **"Ascend Consulting."** It felt right—strong, clear, purposeful. He was ready to ascend.

He was rewriting his narrative, one step at a time.

CHAPTER TWENTY-SEVEN

The Return of the First Bencher

Aniket climbed the narrow staircase to Sahil's workshop, his heart heavy with a mixture of anticipation and anxiety. It had been months since they last met, their lives diverging as both pursued their individual paths. Yet now, standing at the door, Aniket felt a surge of urgency. He needed to reconnect with the one person who had always believed in him, even when he struggled to believe in himself.

The door was slightly ajar, and the familiar sounds of machinery, along with the low hum of voices, drifted into the hallway. Taking a deep breath, he pushed it open and stepped into the lively workshop. The air smelled of oil and metal, and the clinking of tools mixed with the steady whirr of machines filled the space with the pulse of innovation.

Across the room, Aniket saw Sahil hunched over a workbench, assembling a small motor with the intense focus that had always made Aniket proud of his friend. Sahil had come so far, transforming his dreams into something real and impactful. As Aniket stood there watching, hope flickered within him—a reminder that maybe he could still find his own way.

"Sahil?" Aniket called hesitantly, barely audible over the noise.

Sahil looked up, a wide grin spreading across his face. He wiped his hands on a rag and walked over, his eyes lighting up with surprise and joy.

"Aniket!" Sahil exclaimed, pulling him into a bear hug. "It's been ages! What are you doing here? I didn't expect to see you, but it's great that you came!"

Aniket chuckled, the tension in his body easing as he hugged his friend back. "I've missed this place... and you," he admitted.

Sahil stepped back, eyes studying Aniket's face with genuine concern. "I've missed you too, man. How are things? How's your consultancy going?"

Aniket's smile faltered slightly as a wave of doubt washed over him. "It's been... tough. I knew starting something on my own wouldn't be easy, but I feel like I'm just stumbling in the dark, trying to figure it all out."

Sahil nodded; his face thoughtful. "That's how it always feels at the beginning. It's hard because you're stepping into the unknown without a map. But you've made it this far, Aniket. That's something to be proud of."

Aniket shrugged, his gaze wandering around the workshop. The lively energy of Sahil's thriving business felt worlds apart from the solitary hours Aniket spent at his desk. "I don't know, Sahil. Sometimes I feel like I'm just pretending, like I don't really know what I'm doing."

Sahil's expression softened, and his voice held a quiet understanding. "We all feel like that at times. Even now, I have days where I question everything, where I wonder if I'm really cut out for this. But the key is to keep going because you believe in what you're doing. That's what gets you through."

Aniket's heart ached with a mixture of envy and admiration. "You make it sound so easy, but I'm terrified. I'm afraid of failing and losing everything I've worked for."

Sahil's gaze turned serious, his tone firm. "I know that fear, Aniket. I've been there. There were countless moments when I wanted to quit, when I thought I couldn't go on. But every failure, every setback was a lesson. It was still a step forward, even if it didn't feel like it at the time."

Sahil gestured to the bustling workshop around them. "This place? It wasn't built on success alone. It was built on mistakes, failures, and the willingness to keep getting back up. You don't succeed by avoiding failure—you succeed by learning from it."

A lump formed in Aniket's throat, and he blinked back the sting of tears. "How do you keep going, Sahil? How do you push through when it feels like everything is falling apart?"

Sahil paused for a moment; his eyes distant as he reflected on his journey. "I remind myself why I started in the first place. I think about the people who believed in me, the dreams I had, and the difference I wanted to make. When it gets tough, I hold on to that—my purpose. And I keep moving forward, even when it hurts."

He placed a reassuring hand on Aniket's shoulder, his grip steady and confident. "You have that same fire in you, Aniket. You just need to find it again and let it guide you."

Aniket nodded, his heart swelling with gratitude. "Thank you, Sahil. I needed to hear that."

Sahil smiled warmly. "Anytime. Remember, you're not alone. You've got people who believe in you, who are rooting for you."

They stood together for a moment, the noise of the workshop fading as the weight of their friendship anchored Aniket. After months of feeling lost, it was as if he had found a compass again.

"Come on," Sahil said, his voice brightening. "I want to show you something."

He led Aniket through the workshop, weaving between workbenches and machines, exchanging smiles and nods with engineers and technicians. They reached a glass-walled conference room where a group of people were gathered around a table, intently focused on designs and prototypes.

"This," Sahil said, his voice filled with pride, "is our latest project. It's a modular energy system, designed to adapt to different environments—homes, businesses, even off-grid communities. We've been developing it for months, and we're finally bringing it to life."

Aniket's eyes widened as he took in the complex designs spread across the table. "This is incredible, Sahil. I had no idea you were working on something like this."

Sahil's smile widened. "It's been challenging, but this is one of the most rewarding projects we've ever tackled. It's not just about the technology—it's about creating something that makes a real difference, something that helps people live more sustainably."

Aniket felt a surge of admiration for his friend. "You're really making an impact here. It's amazing."

Sahil shrugged, his expression softening. "I'm just following my passion, Aniket. And you can do the same. You have so much knowledge and experience to share. Don't let fear hold you back."

They spent the next few hours talking, brainstorming, and sharing memories of their journeys. For the first time in months, Aniket felt lighter, the weight of his doubts lifting. He realized that he didn't need to have all the answers right away. It was okay to stumble, as long as he kept moving forward.

As the sun dipped below the horizon, casting the workshop in a warm golden light, Aniket knew he had found something far more valuable than just advice. He had rediscovered his sense of purpose. Sahil's belief in him, their connection, had rekindled the spark inside him that had been smothered by fear.

"Thank you, Sahil. For everything," Aniket said, his voice thick with emotion. "You've always believed in me, even when I didn't believe in myself."

Sahil smiled, his eyes shining with warmth. "You're my best friend, Aniket. I've seen what you're capable of, and I know you've got what it takes to make your dreams happen. Just promise me one thing—don't give up."

Aniket nodded, the fear that had gripped him for so long dissolving into a quiet determination. "I won't. I promise."

As they stood together, the sounds of the workshop buzzing around them, Aniket felt an overwhelming sense of clarity. He was ready to face the challenges, to embrace the failures, and to learn from them.

And as he stepped outside into the cool night air, the stars twinkling above, Aniket knew that he was no longer the same person he had been when he first started this journey. He wasn't just the first bencher anymore. He was someone with the courage to rewrite his own story, to follow his own path—no matter where it might lead.

CHAPTER TWENTY-EIGHT

The Gravity of Falling Upward

Aniket sat in his modest office, fingers tapping nervously on the cluttered desk. Papers, notebooks, and a whiteboard filled with hastily scribbled ideas surrounded him. Morning sunlight streamed through the narrow window, casting a warm glow that did little to ease the tension tightening his chest. The ticking clock on the wall seemed louder than usual, each second amplifying the weight of the decision looming before him.

Weeks had passed since his pivotal conversation with Sahil, weeks filled with sleepless nights and relentless days spent reimagining his struggling consultancy. He had been wrestling with how to transform Ascend Consulting into something more aligned with his true passions, something that genuinely utilized his skills and experience to make a meaningful impact.

The fear of taking a misstep, of risking the little he had built, had kept him paralyzed. Yet the greater fear of stagnation, of watching his dreams fade into oblivion, propelled him to this critical juncture. Today, he would decide whether to take a leap into the unknown or remain tethered to a path that no longer inspired him.

His phone vibrated softly on the desk. Seeing Sahil's name flash on the screen brought a mix of comfort and anxiety.

"Hey, Aniket! How's everything going?" Sahil's voice carried its usual warmth and unwavering confidence.

Aniket took a deep breath, steadying himself. "I'm about to make a big change, Sahil. I'm pivoting Ascend Consulting."

There was a brief pause before Sahil replied, his tone encouraging. "That's a bold move. Tell me more."

"I've been reflecting a lot on our last talk," Aniket began, his gaze drifting to the chaotic whiteboard. "I want to shift my focus to helping small businesses and startups with strategic planning and growth. I realize I have a knack for analysing problems and crafting solutions that can really make a difference for them."

"That sounds like a perfect fit for you," Sahil said thoughtfully. "You've always been great at seeing the bigger picture and identifying ways to improve things. But I sense some hesitation. What's on your mind?"

Aniket sighed, leaning back in his chair. "I'm scared, to be honest. What if it doesn't work out? What if I fail again?"

"Failure is part of the journey," Sahil responded gently. "It's not the opposite of success; it's a stepping stone to it. Every setback teaches you something valuable. The only real failure is not trying at all."

"I know you're right," Aniket admitted, his voice barely above a whisper. "But it feels like I'm walking a tightrope without a safety net."

"You're already on that tightrope," Sahil reminded him. "The key is to keep moving forward. And remember, if you stumble, it's not the end. You can always get back up."

Aniket felt a flicker of determination ignite within him. "You're right. I can't let fear hold me back any longer. I need to do this—for myself and for my aspirations."

"I'm proud of you," Sahil said, sincerity evident in his voice. "Taking this step is a victory in itself. And remember, I'm here for you, no matter what."

"Thanks, Sahil. Your support means a lot."

After they ended the call, Aniket sat in contemplative silence. The gravity of his decision pressed upon him, but so did a newfound resolve. He picked up the phone again, this time dialling the number of one of his most challenging clients—a business owner who had been resistant to his previous suggestions.

As the phone rang, each tone seemed to echo louder than the last. His palms grew damp, but he steadied himself.

"Hello?" The voice on the other end was curt, businesslike.

"Hello, this is Aniket Sharma from Ascend Consulting," he began, striving to keep his voice steady. "I'd like to discuss some new strategies that I believe could significantly benefit your business. Would you be open to setting up a meeting?"

There was a moment of silence that felt like an eternity. Then, to his surprise, the client replied, "Alright, let's schedule something for next week."

Relief washed over Aniket. "Thank you. I'll send over some proposed times."

Ending the call, he allowed himself a small smile. It was a modest victory, but a crucial one. He had confronted his fear and taken a decisive step forward.

He rose from his chair and approached the whiteboard. Picking up a marker, he wrote a single word at the top in bold letters: **"Growth."**

Staring at the word, he felt a surge of purpose. This wasn't just about business expansion; it was about personal development, embracing challenges, and learning from every experience—success or failure.

Meanwhile, at the vibrant hub of innovation that was Sahil's workshop, a different kind of challenge was unfolding. Sahil stood at the head of the conference table, facing his team whose faces mirrored a mix of concern and anticipation.

"We've encountered a significant issue," Sahil announced, his voice steady but sombre. "The new material for our modular energy units isn't performing as expected under stress tests. This isn't a complete loss, but it's a serious setback."

A murmur rippled through the room. Rohan, the lead engineer, furrowed his brow. "What are our options? We've invested heavily in this material."

Sahil took a moment before responding, his gaze meeting each team member's eyes. "We need to pivot. Go back to the drawing board, explore alternative materials, and rethink our design where necessary. This isn't the first hurdle we've faced, and it won't be the last. But I have complete faith in our ability to overcome this."

Priya, the project manager, chimed in. "It's disappointing, but we've learned a lot through this process. We can use that knowledge to make the next iteration even better."

"Exactly," Sahil agreed. "Failure isn't a dead end; it's a detour—a chance to discover new paths we might not have considered otherwise."

The team's initial disappointment began to shift toward a renewed sense of purpose. Conversations sparked around the table about potential solutions, new materials to test, and innovative design tweaks.

As the meeting concluded, Sahil felt a swell of pride in his team. Their resilience and adaptability were testaments to the culture they had built together—a culture that didn't shy away from failure but embraced it as an integral part of success.

Returning to his office, Sahil pulled out his phone and sent a message to Aniket:

"Just faced a major setback with our project materials. But we're pushing forward. Remember, every failure is a lesson in disguise. Keep moving ahead."

Aniket received the message just as he was wrapping up his notes for the upcoming client meeting. Reading Sahil's words, he felt a kinship that transcended their individual journeys. Both were navigating the unpredictable terrain of entrepreneurship, confronting obstacles, and learning to view failures not as defeats but as opportunities for growth.

He replied: *"Thanks for sharing. It's encouraging to know we're both tackling challenges head-on. Let's catch up soon."*

Aniket leaned back, reflecting on the day's events. **The gravity of falling upward—of embracing failure as a catalyst for growth—was becoming clearer.** He understood now that setbacks were not indicators of his inadequacy but necessary steps along the path to achieving his goals.

He thought back to his academic years, where being the "first bencher" meant striving for perfection, avoiding mistakes at all costs. But life, he realized, wasn't about flawless execution. It was about resilience, adaptability, and the courage to keep moving forward despite uncertainties.

The road ahead was uncharted and undoubtedly fraught with challenges. But for the first time in a long while, Aniket felt equipped to navigate it—not because he expected smooth sailing, but because he was ready to learn from every twist and turn.

He glanced once more at the word **"Growth"** on his whiteboard. It symbolized more than business objectives; it encapsulated his personal evolution. With renewed determination, he began drafting a proposal for the upcoming meeting, ideas flowing with an ease he hadn't felt in years.

Back at the workshop, Sahil immersed himself in brainstorming sessions with his team. They explored unconventional materials, considered collaborations with research institutions, and even entertained the idea of open-sourcing part of their project to attract fresh perspectives.

Late into the evening, as the team dispersed, Sahil stepped outside. The city lights shimmered under the night sky. He felt a deep sense of fulfilment—not because they had solved the problem yet, but because they were united in their pursuit, undeterred by setbacks.

He thought about the parallels between his journey and Aniket's. Both had chosen paths fraught with uncertainty, both had faced and would continue to face failures. Yet, it was these very challenges that enriched their experiences, pushing them to grow beyond their perceived limits.

Sahil pulled out his phone once more and sent Aniket a final message for the day:

"Remember, it's not about how many times we fall, but how many times we get back up. Proud of the strides you're making."

Aniket, seeing the message pop up on his screen, smiled and felt a warm surge of camaraderie. He replied:

"Couldn't agree more. Here's to embracing the journey, wherever it leads."

The gravity of falling upward was no longer a daunting concept for Aniket. It was a liberating realization that failures were not anchors but stepping stones. Each misstep offered lessons that propelled him closer to his aspirations.

As he prepared for bed, Aniket felt a calm confidence. The fear that had once paralyzed him was giving way to a resilient optimism. He was ready to face whatever came next—not because he expected to succeed without obstacles, but because he understood that every experience, good or bad, was a valuable part of his journey upward.

He turned off the lights, the word **"Growth"** glowing faintly on the whiteboard in the moonlight. And as he drifted into sleep, he carried with him the assurance that he was, indeed, on the right path.

CHAPTER TWENTY-NINE

The Unlearning Process

Aniket sat in his office, the steady hum of the city outside a gentle backdrop as he stared at the notebook on his desk. It was filled with his usual neat handwriting, charts meticulously drawn, strategies carefully thought out. Everything was in order, as it had always been. But as he looked at the pages filled with plans and projections; he felt a strange sense of detachment—a hollow feeling as if all his well-laid plans were somehow incomplete.

The thrill he had felt in recent weeks, the excitement of diving into new ideas and embracing creative risks, seemed to be fading. In its place, the old pressures were resurfacing—the rigid expectations, the urge to control every outcome, the relentless need for measurable success. It was as if the weight of everything he had been taught, everything that had shaped him, was dragging him back into the same pattern of thinking he had worked so hard to break free from.

He let out a long sigh, glancing up at the whiteboard on the wall. It was filled with goals and milestones, timelines that charted a clear, logical path forward for his consultancy. But instead of inspiring him, the sight felt suffocating, like a roadmap that was forcing him back into a mould that no longer fit.

For weeks, he had tried to keep everything on track—success, measured by the numbers. But now, something inside him was asking for more. It wasn't enough to just follow the rules anymore.

His phone buzzed on the desk, breaking his train of thought. Aniket glanced at the screen and saw a message from Sahil:

"How's it going, Aniket? Remember, it's okay to let go of what you think you know. Sometimes, unlearning is just as important as learning."

Aniket stared at the message, his heart lifting slightly. *Unlearning.* It was something Sahil had mentioned to him before, but the concept had always seemed abstract, distant—something he hadn't fully grasped. He had been so focused on learning, on accumulating knowledge, on following the blueprint for success, that he had never considered what it might mean to unlearn, to challenge the very foundation of what he thought he knew.

He closed his eyes, letting his mind drift back to the years he had spent chasing the top of his class, the secure corporate job, the polished resume. All his life, he had been taught to measure success by tangible outcomes—grades, promotions, recognition. It had driven him to excel, but it had also kept him trapped, locked into a narrow definition of achievement. The years of pressure to be perfect, to follow the rules, had led him to where he was now, but they had also left him feeling incomplete.

He opened his eyes, staring at the whiteboard once more. The neatly written plans that had once felt like a source of clarity now felt like shackles—confining him, holding him back from exploring something deeper, something more meaningful.

Aniket stood up slowly, walking over to the whiteboard. His hand hovered over the eraser, hesitation creeping into his chest. It would be so easy to keep going as he had been, to stick to the plan and avoid the discomfort of uncertainty. But something inside him whispered that it was time to let go. He took a deep breath, and with one smooth motion, he wiped the board clean.

The blank surface seemed to reflect the vastness of possibilities before him—a clean slate, unburdened by the weight of expectations and rigid plans. His heart pounded in his chest, but for the first time in a long while, it wasn't out of fear. It was out of excitement.

Picking up the marker, he wrote a single word in the center of the board: *Unlearn.*

Stepping back, he let the word sink in. What would it mean to unlearn? To let go of the need for control, the compulsion to measure everything by success or failure? To trust in the process, even when the path wasn't clear?

He sat back down at his desk, picking up his pen. But this time, the words that flowed onto the page felt different. They weren't about hitting targets or maximizing growth. They were about people, about connection, creativity, and exploration. He wasn't writing for approval or validation anymore; he was writing because it felt true, because it felt right.

As he finished, a sense of calm washed over him. For so long, he had been caught in the pursuit of success as defined by others. Now, for the first time, he felt as though he was on his own path—one that wasn't driven by fear or the need for external approval, but by a deeper sense of purpose.

He picked up his phone, smiling as he typed a quick message to Sahil: *"You're right. It's time to unlearn. Thank you for always being there."*

With a lighter heart, he hit send.

Meanwhile, in his sunlit office overlooking the bustling city, Sahil stood before a group of young entrepreneurs. The room buzzed with excitement; their eyes filled with the spark of possibility. This was the mentorship program he had started—a way to give back, to share the lessons and failures that had shaped his own entrepreneurial journey. Seeing these eager faces reminded him of how far he had come, and how important it was to pass those lessons on.

Sahil took a deep breath, letting the moment settle before he began. "Thank you all for being here today. I'm honoured to have the opportunity to share my journey with you, to talk about the lessons I've learned, the mistakes I've made, and the things I wish I had known when I was in your shoes."

There were nods of anticipation, murmurs of excitement. Sahil smiled as he continued, "I want to start by talking about failure—because it's something you're all going to face, probably more times than you can count. It's tough, especially when you're putting everything on the line for your dream. But failure isn't the end of the road. It's part of the process. It's not something to fear, but something to embrace."

A hand shot up from the back of the room—a young woman with bright eyes and a determined expression. "How do you deal with failure, Sahil Sir? How do you keep going when everything seems like it's falling apart?"

Sahil smiled softly, appreciating the question. "It's all about perspective. When you face a setback, it's easy to feel like everything you've built is crumbling. But if you can take a step back and see the bigger picture, you'll realize that failure is just a step on the journey. It's not an end; it's a lesson."

He paused, his voice softening. "It's about resilience. It's about the courage to get back up, even when it's hard. To believe in your dream, in what you're building, even when the world tells you it's not possible."

More nods of understanding rippled through the room, and Sahil felt the connection deepening. He continued, "But there's something else that's just as important: unlearning. We're taught to fear failure, to see it as proof that we're not good enough. But that's not the truth. The truth is that failure is just part of growth."

Another hand went up—a young man with a thoughtful look. "What exactly do you mean by unlearning?"

Sahil's eyes lit up. "Unlearning is about letting go of the beliefs and habits that keep us from taking risks. It's about questioning the narratives we've been handed—the ones that tell us success looks a certain way, or that failure is something to avoid. It's about finding your own truth and your own path."

He glanced around the room, feeling proud of these young dreamers, who were willing to take risks and challenge the status quo. "Unlearning isn't easy. It takes time and a lot of self-awareness. But once you start, you'll discover a freedom you never knew was possible—a freedom to create, to explore, to fail, and to grow."

The group murmured with agreement; their excitement palpable. For Sahil, this was what success was about—not just achieving milestones but inspiring others to find their own path.

That evening, as the city's lights twinkled against the darkening sky, Sahil sat at his desk, reflecting on the day. He glanced at his phone and saw Aniket's message: *"You're right, Sahil. It's time to unlearn. Thank you for always being there."*

Sahil smiled, his heart swelling with pride for his friend. He quickly typed back: *"You're doing amazing, Aniket. Keep going. The best is yet to come."*

As he hit send, Sahil leaned back in his chair, his mind drifting back to the young entrepreneurs he had spoken with earlier that day. It reminded him how important it was to give others the courage to unlearn, to let go of the fears and expectations that held them back.

Because sometimes, the greatest journey wasn't in accumulating knowledge, but in letting go of the things that no longer served you—in finding the courage to rewrite your own story.

And as Sahil looked out at the city, a deep sense of satisfaction settled over him. They were all on their own paths, learning and unlearning, finding new ways to create, to fail, and to succeed.

And in that, they would all grow.

CHAPTER THIRTY

The Rebirth of Creativity

Aniket sat quietly at his desk, his eyes closed, hands resting on the smooth wooden surface. The early morning light filtered through the window, casting a soft glow across the room, and the faint hum of the city waking up reached his ears. He took a deep breath, savouring the calmness, his mind clear and heart steady. Today felt different—lighter, filled with anticipation that had eluded him for months. It was a new day, a fresh start.

For too long, the consultancy had been on shaky ground. Growth was slow, inconsistent, and Aniket had become trapped in an endless cycle of self-doubt and fear. Every step forward felt fragile, and every challenge made him hesitate, afraid of risking what little stability he had. But something had changed over the past few weeks. Conversations with Sahil, late nights reflecting on his path, and staring at the blank pages of his notebook made Aniket realize something crucial: his fear of failure was holding him back from embracing the full potential of his creativity.

Opening his eyes, he smiled to himself and reached for the notebook on his desk. The pages were filled with ideas, sketches, and plans he had been too scared to pursue. He had been so consumed by what could go wrong that he had forgotten the thrill of imagining what could go right. Today, though, was different.

He flipped through the pages with renewed energy, feeling a surge of excitement bubble up inside him. For the first time in a long while, he wasn't paralyzed by uncertainty. He was inspired. Picking up his pen, his heart began to pound in sync with the racing thoughts in his head. Ideas flowed effortlessly, filling the pages with concepts he had once been too hesitant to consider. He wrote about the businesses he wanted to help, the challenges they faced, and the strategic approaches that could guide them toward sustainable growth.

But this time, it wasn't just about the numbers or profitability. Aniket found himself focusing on creativity—the joy of finding new ways to solve old problems. He embraced risk, thinking outside the box and exploring opportunities that scared him in the past.

Hours passed in a blur, the pen moving in a near-constant flurry of motion as his mind danced with possibilities. The excitement of creation had taken hold, and Aniket was lost in it—fully immersed, forgetting the world around him. When he finally paused to look at the notebook filled with his passionate, hurried scrawl, a wave of pride washed over him. This was the moment he had been searching for.

The clock on the wall caught his eye. He blinked in disbelief—it was already past noon. The entire morning had vanished without him noticing, lost in the current of creativity that had swept him away. His stomach growled, reminding him he hadn't eaten, but the gnawing hunger didn't matter. He felt more alive than he had in years, more energized by the work than he ever could have imagined.

His phone buzzed, pulling him back to the present. Seeing Sahil's name, Aniket smiled as he answered.

"Hey, Sahil!" he said, his voice bright with excitement. "You won't believe the morning I've had."

Sahil's warm laugh filled the line. "Sounds like there's been a breakthrough. Tell me everything."

Aniket leaned back in his chair, glancing at the notebook overflowing with fresh ideas. "I've been writing nonstop. It's like a flood of ideas that I didn't even know I had. I'm planning new strategies for the consultancy, but more than that, I feel like I've finally let go of my fear of failure. I'm seeing everything differently—embracing the uncertainty, the risks, the excitement of creating something new. It feels incredible."

Sahil's pride was palpable. "That's amazing, Aniket. I knew you had this in you. Creativity isn't just for artists or inventors. It's about how you approach everything—work, life, problems. It's about finding joy in the process, in the risks. That's where the magic happens."

Aniket nodded, his heart swelling with gratitude. "You're right. I've been so caught up in trying to avoid mistakes that I forgot why I started this in the first place. But now, I feel like I'm looking at everything with fresh eyes. I'm ready to take risks, to try new things. It's like I've been asleep for so long, and I'm finally waking up."

Sahil's voice softened, filled with encouragement. "That's the spirit. You can't grow without taking risks. Failure isn't the enemy. It's just another teacher. Each mistake, each setback is an opportunity to learn something new. You're building something amazing, Aniket. You just have to trust yourself and enjoy the process."

"Thank you, Sahil," Aniket said, his voice steady, filled with emotion. "You've been an inspiration. Watching you build your business, seeing how you face challenges with resilience—it's given me the courage to do the same."

Sahil's laughter was light, filled with warmth. "You're stronger than you give yourself credit for, Aniket. You've always had this in you. Now that you're embracing it, there's no stopping you. I can't wait to see what you create."

Their conversation flowed easily after that, filled with laughter and dreams for the future. When they finally hung up, Aniket felt a deep sense of peace. He turned back to his notebook, his mind still buzzing with ideas, ready to continue the creative flow.

He knew the path ahead wouldn't be smooth. Challenges would come, failures would still test him, but now he understood something fundamental—he didn't have to fear failure. Instead, he could welcome it, learn from it, and use it to propel himself forward. This wasn't just about building a business anymore. It was about rediscovering his passion, his creativity, and most importantly, the joy that came from creating something meaningful.

Sahil, meanwhile, found himself stepping into the large conference room of his newly expanded office. The room was filled with investors, journalists, and industry leaders, all eagerly awaiting the presentation that could cement his company's reputation as an industry leader. The air was thick with anticipation, but Sahil felt calm. After years of hard work and countless hurdles, today marked a milestone—a moment that brought his team's vision to life.

As he glanced around the room, his eyes caught the familiar faces of his team—people who had been there from the beginning, who had believed in his dream even when the journey seemed uncertain. Their unwavering support, their collective effort, had brought them to this point, and Sahil's heart swelled with pride.

Stepping up to the podium, he took a deep breath before addressing the room. "Thank you all for being here today," he began, his voice calm and clear. "What you're about to see is the culmination of years of research, innovation, and determination. But more than that, it's a testament to the power of creativity, resilience, and the willingness to push beyond what we thought was possible."

A sleek, modern machine appeared on the large screen behind him, its design both elegant and functional. Sahil continued, "This is our new modular energy system. A product we believe will revolutionize how we approach energy—how we live, work, and interact with our environment."

Excited murmurs spread through the audience, and Sahil smiled as he felt the energy in the room shift. He knew this wasn't just about showcasing new technology. It was about showing the world that creativity, risk, and innovation were the keys to progress.

"This product isn't just the result of technological advancement," he added, his voice growing more passionate. "It's the result of creative thinking—of looking at old problems in new ways, of taking risks, and embracing failure as part of the growth process. Every setback we faced led us to this moment."

The crowd erupted into applause, and Sahil felt a deep sense of accomplishment. They had created something extraordinary, something that would change the industry. But more than that, they had proved that creativity and resilience were the true drivers of success.

As the presentation concluded and the crowd dispersed, Sahil found himself surrounded by enthusiastic investors and curious journalists. But his thoughts drifted back to his earlier conversation with Aniket. Pulling out his phone, he quickly typed a message:

"You're on the right path, Aniket. Keep following your passion and embracing the risks. You're creating something incredible, and I'm proud of you."

Aniket read Sahil's message as he sat at his desk, looking at the words he had written on his whiteboard earlier that morning:

"Creativity is not about perfection. It's about the willingness to take risks, to make mistakes, and to embrace failure as part of the process."

He smiled, feeling the truth of those words settle deep within him. For so long, he had chased perfection, fearing every misstep. But now, he understood that real creativity—the kind that leads to innovation and growth—thrives in imperfection. It flourishes when we're willing to step into the unknown, to take bold risks, and to learn from every fall.

Picking up his pen, Aniket added another line beneath the first:

"In that willingness to embrace failure, we find the freedom to create, to dream, and to grow."

Setting the pen down, he felt a deep sense of fulfilment. The rebirth of his creativity wasn't just about coming up with new ideas or strategies for his consultancy. It was about embracing the process, about finding joy in the risks, the uncertainties, and the moments of inspiration that came when he let go of fear.

As the city lights began to twinkle outside his window, casting a soft glow over the room, Aniket knew that he was finally on the right path. He had rediscovered the passion and creativity that had sparked his journey in the first place. He was no longer holding back, no longer afraid to fail.

This was his rebirth—a new chapter in his life where creativity, passion, and risk-taking would guide him forward. And no matter what came next, he was ready.

Because he was awake. He was alive. He was free to create, to dream, and to grow.

And that was more than enough.

CHAPTER THIRTY-ONE

The Reunion

The banquet hall buzzed with life, the air thick with laughter, clinking glasses, and the hum of old friends reconnecting. Soft lighting illuminated the room, casting a warm glow over the elegantly set tables adorned with white linens and floral centerpieces. Aniket lingered near the entrance, his heart racing as he took it all in. The years since his last contact with most of his classmates had stretched long, making this moment both exhilarating and daunting.

The idea of coming to this reunion had felt like a gamble. He had almost stayed away, unsure if he was ready to answer the inevitable questions—questions about his life, his choices, his work, and whether he had achieved success by anyone's standard, including his own. Yet something had urged him to show up. Maybe it was the need to see how much he had grown, to understand how far he had come, or maybe just the curiosity to see the faces of those who had shared his past.

Aniket's eyes scanned the room. He spotted Rohan at the bar, now with strands of grey in his hair, laughing heartily with a group of people. Across the room, Priyanka held court in a lively conversation, her voice rising above the rest, just as it had back in school. Everywhere Aniket looked, familiar faces reappeared—faces those stirred memories of youth and ambition, of dreams not yet shaped by the reality of life.

Taking a deep breath, he approached the registration table where a cheerful woman handed out name tags. When she handed him his, it felt oddly heavy for something so small.

"Aniket Sharma," she read out with a smile. "It's been a long time! Welcome back."

He smiled politely, nodding. "Yes, it has. Thank you."

He pinned the tag to his shirt, grounding himself with the simple act. It made him feel like he belonged again, even if just for the evening. Whatever emotions the night held, he was here, ready to face it.

As he walked into the main hall, the noise of overlapping conversations faded into the background. Groups of people clustered together, swapping stories and laughter, reminiscing about days gone by. It was comforting in one sense, but also disorienting—like stepping back in time, yet feeling the weight of the years that had passed.

"Aniket!" A familiar voice broke through the noise, and he turned to see Rohan approaching with a broad smile. "Man, it's been too long! How are you?"

Aniket grinned, his anxiety momentarily melting away at the sight of his old friend. "I'm good, Rohan. Really good. You haven't changed much."

Rohan laughed, glancing at his greying hair. "I don't know about that, but I'll take the compliment. What about you? I heard you started your own consultancy. How's that going?"

Aniket paused, his mind racing for the right words. "It's been... an adventure. Lots of ups and downs, challenges I didn't expect. But I'm learning a lot. It's fulfilling, in its own way."

Rohan nodded knowingly. "That's the thing about starting something on your own. It's always harder than it looks, but the fact that you took the leap? That's huge. Most people wouldn't have the guts."

Aniket felt a warmth spread through him at Rohan's words—a validation he hadn't realized he needed. "Thanks. That really means a lot."

They continued talking, reminiscing about old times, the conversation flowing easily. It felt good to return to these shared memories, to laugh about their younger selves, as though reconnecting with a part of himself he had forgotten. Yet, amidst the comfort of it all, Aniket couldn't shake a growing sense of unease—an unfinished feeling, a search for something or someone else.

His eyes drifted over the crowd, searching for the face he hadn't yet seen—the one he had been hoping would be here.

And then, he spotted him.

Sahil stood near the stage, surrounded by a small group of people, gesturing animatedly as he spoke. He looked every bit the successful entrepreneur he had become—confident, comfortable in his own skin, with the energy of someone who had found his rhythm in life.

Aniket felt a familiar mix of emotions wash over him—admiration, pride, but also envy. Sahil had faced his share of challenges, setbacks, and failures, but he had emerged stronger each time. Still, underneath the envy, there was an undeniable sense of respect for his friend, a realization that Sahil had been one of the few constants in his life, always encouraging him to keep pushing forward.

Taking a deep breath, Aniket made his way across the room, weaving through the crowd. As he approached, Sahil's eyes lifted, and when their gazes met, a wide smile broke across his face.

"Aniket!" Sahil's voice rang out, warm and genuine, as he pulled Aniket into a hug. "I was hoping you'd come. It's been way too long."

Aniket returned the hug, feeling a lump form in his throat. "It's good to see you, Sahil. You look... well, you look incredible."

Sahil chuckled, his eyes crinkling with amusement. "Thanks. But enough about me. How have you been? How's the consultancy?"

Aniket hesitated, the old familiar doubt creeping back. He wondered briefly if he measured up to the man standing in front of him. But then he remembered the conversations they'd had, how Sahil had always believed in him, even when he hadn't believed in himself.

"It's been challenging," he admitted, his voice steady. "I've had to unlearn a lot of things—especially the idea that success means having everything figured out. But I'm finding my way. It's been freeing, in a way I never expected."

Sahil's expression softened, his eyes reflecting deep understanding. "That's huge, Aniket. It takes real courage to let go of old expectations and do things your way. I'm proud of you, man."

Aniket felt a surge of gratitude. "Thank you. You've been such an inspiration—watching you build your business, handle setbacks, and still keep moving forward. It's made me realize I don't have to have all the answers right now. I can just... keep going."

Sahil smiled, his voice gentle. "You've always had it in you. You just needed to believe it. And now, look at you. You're making it happen."

For a moment, they stood in silence, the rest of the room falling away as they reconnected—two friends on different paths, but bound by shared experiences, by the struggles and the triumphs that had shaped them.

"Come on," Sahil said with a grin, his eyes sparkling with excitement. "There are so many people who want to hear about what you've been up to."

Aniket felt a flicker of anxiety rise, but he pushed it aside. With Sahil at his side, the fear of judgment faded. He nodded. "Alright, let's go."

They made their way through the crowd, stopping to talk with old friends. Aniket found himself laughing more easily, sharing stories, and reconnecting with people he hadn't seen in years. And with each conversation, each exchange of memories and experiences, Aniket felt a sense of peace wash over him—an acknowledgment that he didn't need to prove anything to anyone. He was on his journey, and that was enough.

As the night wore on, the laughter turned reflective, the conversations deepened. Aniket spoke to people who had taken wildly different paths—some more traditional, some more daring—but what struck him wasn't the success or failure in their stories. It was the shared humanity in the struggle, the lessons learned along the way, and the person each of them had become.

He stood by the bar, a glass of water in hand, watching as Sahil animatedly spoke to a group of people. Aniket felt a wave of pride for his friend—not because of his success, but because of his resilience, his ability to face failure head-on, and his courage to keep going despite the obstacles.

Aniket took a deep breath, his heart steady as the realization settled over him: he was no longer chasing the image of success he once thought he needed. He was building a life on his terms—one that allowed for mistakes, for growth, and for joy in the journey itself.

And as the night deepened, with music and laughter filling the air, Aniket knew he was exactly where he needed to be.

This reunion wasn't just with old friends—it was a reunion with himself. A reunion with the person he was becoming, one step, one failure, one success at a time.

CHAPTER THIRTY-TWO

Beyond the Comfort Zone

Aniket stood at the front of the small conference room, his heart hammering in his chest. Before him sat a group of business owners and aspiring entrepreneurs, each looking at him with curiosity and expectation. The glow from the projector bathed the room in soft light, highlighting the words on the screen behind him: **"Strategic Growth and Innovation."**

He wiped his clammy hands on the sides of his trousers and took a deep breath, attempting to calm the nerves that had been building all morning. This was his first major workshop, an ambitious step forward that he had been planning for months. It was a chance to offer guidance to small businesses and startups, to help them navigate the complexities of growth, risk, and innovation. But it was also a leap into the unknown—one that had filled him with both excitement and anxiety.

As he glanced around the room, he could feel the weight of expectation—his own, as well as that of those sitting before him. Every detail of this presentation had been meticulously crafted, every slide rehearsed, every concept refined. Yet now, standing here, those old familiar doubts began to creep in, whispers of failure reminding him of how easy it was to falter.

But then he remembered Sahil's words, the endless encouragement from his friend who had always believed in him. Sahil had been there every step of the way, telling him that the only real failure was in not trying at all. Aniket exhaled slowly and allowed that thought to center him.

"Good morning, everyone," he began, his voice a little shaky but gaining strength. "Thank you for being here today. I'm Aniket Sharma, and I'm excited to share with you some strategies for navigating the complexities of business growth and innovation."

A murmur of polite acknowledgment rippled through the room, along with nods of encouragement. Aniket latched onto those subtle signs, using them to bolster his confidence. He began the presentation, delving into market analysis, strategic planning, and the critical need for flexibility in an ever-evolving business landscape. The words flowed effortlessly at first, and with each passing minute, he felt a surge of confidence, as though he had found his rhythm.

But as he moved into a more technical section—discussing operational scaling and risk management—he noticed a shift in the room. Some audience members seemed puzzled, their expressions hinting at confusion rather than engagement. Aniket's heart skipped a beat as panic began to rise. He had misjudged his audience. He had veered too deep into the technical details, forgetting that these were small business owners, not corporate executives looking for high-level strategy.

For a moment, he stood frozen. The silence stretched out, each second feeling like an eternity as his mind raced to recover, to pull himself back from the brink of losing them completely. The old insecurities rushed in, the fear that he wasn't cut out for this, that he had overreached, rising in his throat.

But then, he took a deep breath and reminded himself of everything he had learned about adaptability, about how failure was part of the process. The tension in his shoulders eased as he decided to meet the challenge head-on.

"I see some of you looking a bit lost," he said with a self-deprecating smile, his voice softening. "I think I may have gotten a little too technical. Let's take a step back and break this down in simpler terms."

A few chuckles rippled through the audience, and the tension in the room began to dissolve. Aniket adjusted his approach, simplifying the concepts and using relatable case studies to make his points clearer. He could see the shift happening in real time—faces that had been blank or puzzled now nodded in understanding. The atmosphere lightened, and Aniket knew he was back on track.

The rest of the workshop flowed smoothly. The Q&A session afterward was thoughtful and engaging, with participants eager to dive into their own challenges and ask for his advice. Aniket felt a wave of relief and satisfaction wash over him. The workshop had been far from perfect, but he had adapted, recovered, and, most importantly, connected with his audience in a meaningful way.

As the participants filed out of the room, a few stayed behind to chat with him.

"Thank you for the workshop, Aniket," one woman said, her voice sincere. "I've been struggling with scaling my business, and your advice really resonated with me. I feel like I have a much clearer direction now."

Aniket smiled, feeling a swell of pride. "I'm so glad to hear that. If you ever need any more help, feel free to reach out."

She nodded gratefully, her eyes shining with appreciation. "I will, definitely."

As she walked away, Aniket stood still for a moment, reflecting on what had just transpired. He hadn't delivered a flawless presentation, and he hadn't dazzled everyone with effortless brilliance. But he had faced his fears, pushed beyond his comfort zone, and in the end, made a difference for at least a few people. That, he realized, was what mattered most.

He began packing up his things, already thinking about how he could improve for next time. His mind buzzed with new ideas, possibilities for future workshops, and ways to continue growing and learning. The experience had tested him, but he had come out stronger—and that filled him with a quiet, deep-seated satisfaction.

He glanced at his phone and saw a message from Sahil:

"Just took the leap into international markets. There's a lot at stake, but I'm excited. Keep pushing, my friend. The only limits are the ones we set for ourselves."

Aniket smiled as he read the message. Sahil had always been pushing the boundaries, always striving for more, and his latest venture was no different. It was a reminder that growth and risk were intertwined, and that the path to success was never a straight line.

Meanwhile, in the sleek, glass-walled office of his rapidly expanding company, Sahil stood at the head of the conference room table, his heart racing with anticipation. Around him, a group of executives sat, their eyes trained on him as he outlined the next phase of the company's growth: international expansion.

"We've done our research, and the timing is right," Sahil said, his voice steady despite the magnitude of what he was proposing. "We're entering Southeast Asia first. It's a dynamic, growing market, and if we play our cards right, we can establish a foothold there that will allow us to expand further."

The room was filled with murmurs of agreement, nods of excitement, and the energy was electric. Sahil's team had been with him through countless challenges, setbacks, and victories, and now they were on the verge of something monumental.

"We may do mistakes," Sahil continued, his tone serious. "This won't be easy. There will be risks, setbacks—things we can't predict. But we've faced challenges before, and we've always come out stronger."

As the team began to strategize, offering their thoughts and ideas, Sahil felt a surge of pride. They were a cohesive unit, driven by shared goals and the relentless pursuit of excellence. It wasn't just about numbers or profits—it was about building something that mattered.

He paused for a moment, thinking about Aniket. His friend had come so far, had faced his own set of fears and failures, but had never stopped moving forward. Sahil pulled out his phone and quickly typed a message:

"Remember, the only real failure is in not trying. Keep pushing, my friend. There's so much more ahead."

Back in his small office, Aniket read Sahil's message and felt a familiar warmth fill his chest. He stood up and walked over to the whiteboard, where the remnants of his previous planning still lingered. Grabbing the marker, he wrote a single word at the top of the board:

"Ambition."

It felt right, almost like a promise to himself. He had taken a step beyond his comfort zone today, had faced failure, learned from it, and emerged stronger. And now, standing here, he felt ready for the next challenge—the next leap forward.

The journey wasn't about perfection. It was about growth, about continuously pushing the limits of what he thought possible. It was about embracing the discomfort, the risk, and the inevitable setbacks that came with stepping into the unknown.

As he stared at the word on the board, his heart filled with quiet determination. He knew there would be more failures ahead, more moments of doubt, but he also knew that those moments were part of the process. They were stepping stones on the path to something greater.

With a deep breath, Aniket sat back down at his desk, ready to tackle whatever came next. Beyond the comfort zone lay infinite possibilities, and he was ready to embrace them, one step at a time.

Because, in the end, true success wasn't about avoiding failure—it was about having the courage to keep going, no matter what.

CHAPTER THIRTY-THREE

Building the Future

Aniket sat at his desk, the hum of activity around him a reminder of how far he had come. The once small and cluttered office had transformed into a bustling hub of creativity and collaboration. The walls, now adorned with motivational quotes and strategic roadmaps, were a testament to the journey he had taken—the risks, the failures, and the hard-won lessons. Each day felt like a new chapter in a story he was writing, a story about resilience, persistence, and the relentless pursuit of growth.

He glanced at the whiteboard, where a detailed schedule of client meetings and workshops was scribbled in his usual neat handwriting. His consultancy, which had once been a fragile dream, had blossomed. Clients came steadily, referrals grew, and his reputation as a strategic thinker and creative problem-solver was spreading throughout the business community.

But this journey wasn't just about professional success. What Aniket cherished most was the sense of fulfilment—helping businesses innovate and grow while rediscovering his own potential along the way. He had built something meaningful, something real. Every lesson, every risk, every small victory had brought him to this moment.

He picked up his phone, scrolling through his list of clients, ready to start the day's work. But before he could make his first call, his assistant, Meera, stepped into the room, her face beaming with excitement.

"Aniket Sir, there's someone here to see you," she said, her voice tinged with anticipation. "It's Mr. Singh from TechSolutions. He says he's interested in partnering with us for their new product launch."

Aniket's heart skipped a beat. TechSolutions was a major player in the tech industry, known for pushing the boundaries of innovation. Securing a partnership with them would be a game-changer. It was the kind of opportunity he had been working toward for years.

"Please, show him in," Aniket replied, his voice calm despite the excitement surging within him. He stood, straightening his shirt, and taking a deep breath as he prepared himself for the meeting.

When Mr. Singh entered, his presence was commanding yet professional. He scanned the office with curious eyes before offering a firm handshake. "Thank you for seeing me on such short notice, Aniket. I've heard a lot about your work, and I must say, I'm impressed."

Aniket returned the handshake with a steady grip, masking the surge of pride those words ignited. "The pleasure is mine, Mr. Singh.

Mr. Singh took a seat and leaned forward slightly; his tone thoughtful. "We're launching a new product next quarter, something that we believe will disrupt the market. But we need a partner who can help us navigate the complexities of the launch. We need someone who thinks strategically, creatively, and understands the tech industry's unique challenges."

Aniket felt the thrill of possibility stirring within him as he began to imagine the strategies and innovations that could set TechSolutions apart. "I'd be honoured to collaborate with you on this," he said, maintaining a professional demeanour despite his inner excitement. "Could you share more about the product and what you're envisioning for the launch?"

For the next hour, the conversation flowed effortlessly. They discussed market positioning, target demographics, potential roadblocks, and innovative approaches to branding and marketing. Aniket thrived in the exchange, drawing on his deep well of experience while letting his creative instincts guide the conversation.

By the end of the meeting, Mr. Singh sat back in his chair, his expression one of satisfaction. "You've exceeded my expectations, Aniket. You clearly understand the market, and your approach is exactly what we're looking for. I think this is the beginning of a very fruitful partnership."

A rush of accomplishment washed over Aniket, but he remained composed. "Thank you, Mr. Singh. I'm excited about the possibilities, and I'm confident we can create something exceptional together."

They shook hands, and as Mr. Singh left, Aniket sat back at his desk, feeling a sense of pride that was hard to describe. This was the moment he had been working toward—validating all the risks he had taken, the failures he had learned from, and the lessons he had internalized. The partnership with TechSolutions represented not just professional success, but a culmination of his personal growth as well.

Before diving into the next steps, he picked up his phone and typed a quick message to Sahil.

"Just secured a partnership with TechSolutions. Your lessons are paying off. Thank you for always believing in me."

He hit send, a small smile playing on his lips as he imagined Sahil's reaction. There was still much to be done, but Aniket felt ready for whatever challenges came next. He was no longer just building a business—he was building a legacy.

Across the city, in a sprawling, modern office, Sahil stood in front of a massive window overlooking the bustling streets below. The company he had started in a small workshop had grown into a global enterprise, and the headquarters buzzed with the energy of innovation and ambition. Yet even amidst all the success, Sahil never lost sight of the hard-fought battles it took to get here—the failures, the doubts, the relentless perseverance.

The journey had been anything but linear, but that was the beauty of it. Every setback had been an opportunity to learn, to innovate, and to build something even stronger. Now, standing on the brink of yet another expansion, Sahil felt the same excitement he had when he first started—only now, the stakes were higher, and the vision grander.

He turned his gaze away from the window and focused on the large screen behind him, where a map displayed his company's global reach. They had made significant inroads in markets across Asia, Europe, and North America. But now, new frontiers beckoned. Sahil knew this was just the beginning.

His phone buzzed, and when he saw Aniket's message, a wide smile spread across his face. Pride swelled within him as he read the words, knowing that Aniket had always had the potential—he just needed the right encouragement to see it through. He quickly typed a reply.

"That's incredible, Aniket! I always knew you could do it. Keep pushing, keep innovating. The future is yours to build."

He hit send and pocketed the phone, turning his focus back to the task at hand. In the conference room, his senior management team waited, eager to hear his strategy for their next bold move.

"Thank you all for being here," Sahil began, his voice steady and commanding. "We've made tremendous strides in recent years, but now it's time to take the next step. Today, we'll be discussing our expansion into Africa and South America—two regions brimming with untapped potential."

The room buzzed with energy. Sahil could see the excitement and anticipation on the faces of his team. They had been with him through thick and thin, believing in his vision even when the path was uncertain. Together, they had built something remarkable.

"We'll need to adapt our strategies," Sahil continued, "and we'll face challenges unique to these regions. But I believe in our ability to innovate and succeed. We have the talent, the resilience, and the passion to make it happen."

The team began discussing strategies, the room alive with brainstorming, questions, and ideas. Sahil's heart swelled with pride as he watched his team engage, their minds buzzing with possibilities. This was more than just business—it was about building the future, about creating something that would make a lasting impact.

After the meeting, Sahil lingered for a moment, reflecting on how far they had come. He glanced at his phone once more, thinking of Aniket. They were both on different paths, yet in many ways, they were walking the same journey—building, growing, learning.

Later that evening, as Aniket sat at his desk reviewing the plans for his new partnership with TechSolutions, he felt a sense of fulfilment that went beyond mere success. It wasn't just about securing a lucrative deal—it was about the joy of creating something meaningful, of helping others grow, and of applying the lessons he had learned over the years.

He glanced at the whiteboard on his office wall. Written in bold letters was the word "Ambition," a reminder of the vision he had set for himself. But now, it felt incomplete.

He picked up a marker and added a few more words beneath it:

"Building the future, one step, one lesson, one success at a time."

Stepping back, Aniket smiled. The future was wide open, full of challenges and triumphs yet to come. And he was ready for it, knowing that no matter what, he had the tools, the mindset, and the courage to keep moving forward.

Because building the future wasn't just about achieving success. It was about the journey—the risks, the lessons, the resilience. It was about believing in yourself and in what you were creating.

And in that belief, Aniket knew he was unstoppable.

CHAPTER THIRTY-FOUR

The Chains of Success

Aniket sat in his office, staring blankly at the spreadsheet on his laptop screen. The numbers glowed with success—revenue growth, profit margins, client retention rates—all signs that his consultancy was thriving. By all outward measures, he had achieved what he had set out to do. Yet, despite the figures that should have filled him with pride, an unfamiliar sense of unease gnawed at him, leaving a void that success alone couldn't fill.

Over the past few months, his business had expanded rapidly. He had secured larger clients, hired new staff, and even diversified the services his consultancy offered. By most standards, these were enviable milestones. And yet, with each new achievement, the weight of responsibility seemed to grow heavier on his shoulders. The higher the numbers climbed, the more he found himself questioning the cost of maintaining that upward trajectory.

He leaned back in his chair, letting his gaze drift toward the window. Outside, the city skyline gleamed in the golden afternoon light, a stark contrast to the murky thoughts swirling inside him. He had come so far, overcome so many challenges. Yet now, on the cusp of something even greater, he felt an unexpected pull—a temptation he hadn't anticipated.

The buzzing of his phone snapped him out of his thoughts. Glancing at the screen, he saw the name of one of his largest clients: Mr. Verma from a multinational corporation that had recently offered him a long-term contract. The offer promised not just financial stability but also industry recognition—everything an entrepreneur could dream of. But it also came with strings attached, the most binding of which was a commitment to focus almost exclusively on this one client, leaving little room for the smaller businesses and startups that had become the heart of his consultancy's mission.

Aniket hesitated for a moment, then picked up the phone, the knot in his stomach tightening as he did.

"Hello, Mr. Verma. It's good to hear from you."

"Hello, Aniket," came the smooth, confident voice on the other end. "I wanted to follow up on our discussion about the contract. We're ready to move forward, but we need your commitment. This could be a great opportunity for both of us, and we'd like to finalize the details soon."

Aniket felt a wave of tension wash over him. The offer was tempting—security, resources, and a long-term partnership with one of the biggest players in the industry. But the price? His freedom, his ability to pursue the projects that aligned with his passion and creativity.

"I understand, Mr. Verma," he said, trying to keep his voice steady. "It's a significant opportunity, and I'm honoured by your confidence in my consultancy. I'll need a little more time to ensure we can meet your expectations fully."

Mr. Verma's tone softened, his voice almost coaxing. "Aniket, I know it's a big decision. But think about the future. This contract will secure your place in the industry, give you the resources to expand. It's the kind of stability most entrepreneurs dream of."

As Mr. Verma's words echoed in his ear, Aniket felt the pull of temptation grow stronger, whispering promises of comfort, of financial safety. But at the same time, something deep inside resisted—the fire that had driven him from the very start, a fire that refused to be extinguished by the allure of security.

"I'll get back to you soon, Mr. Verma," he said finally, his voice firm. "I just need to make sure it's the right move for both of us."

They exchanged pleasantries, and as Aniket hung up, the weight of the decision pressed down on him like an invisible burden. He had prided himself on building a business that was true to his vision—one that thrived on creativity, flexibility, and the freedom to work with a diverse range of clients. But now, faced with the allure of financial stability, he felt his sense of purpose begin to blur, the lines between ambition and compromise growing faint.

He stood up abruptly, his pulse quickening as he began pacing the office. His thoughts raced between two conflicting desires: the need for growth and security, and the fear of losing the essence of what he had built. The consultancy was more than just a business—it was an extension of himself, of his values, his passion. But how could he balance that against the promise of a secure future?

Only one person came to mind, someone who had always guided him through moments of doubt.

He reached for his phone and dialled Sahil's number, his fingers trembling slightly. The phone rang twice before Sahil's warm, familiar voice answered.

"Aniket! What's going on, my friend? You sound like you've got the weight of the world on your shoulders."

Aniket let out a breath he didn't realize he'd been holding, the tension easing just slightly. "I feel like I am, Sahil. I've been offered a long-term contract with one of my biggest clients, and it's a huge opportunity. But... it would mean shifting almost all my focus to them. I'd have to give up a lot of the freedom I've worked so hard to build."

Sahil's voice became thoughtful, grounding. "It sounds like a tempting offer. But I can tell you're not sure. What's really bothering you?"

Aniket's thoughts spilled out in a rush. "I'm afraid, Sahil. Afraid of losing the business I've built, of getting trapped in a situation that doesn't align with my vision. But at the same time, I'm scared of passing up this opportunity. What if I never get another one like it? What if the business can't grow without it?"

Sahil was quiet for a moment, then he sighed, a sound filled with empathy. "I know where you're coming from. Success can be its own kind of trap. It's easy to be seduced by security, especially when it's right there in front of you. But the question you have to ask yourself is, what kind of success do you want? Is it the stability of one big contract, or the freedom to keep building on your own terms?"

Aniket felt a pang of realization, guilt mixing with doubt. "I don't know, Sahil. I want to secure the business, to provide for my team, to keep growing. But I also don't want to lose what makes this work meaningful to me."

Sahil's voice softened, filled with the wisdom of someone who had faced similar crossroads. "Aniket, the chains of success can be just as binding as the fear of failure. Don't let security become a cage. The freedom to build something meaningful, something that reflects your vision—that's priceless. You have to decide if this contract aligns with that vision or if it's pulling you away from it."

Aniket nodded, even though Sahil couldn't see him. "You're right. I've been so focused on the numbers and growth that I forgot to check if I'm still on the path I set out on. I need to trust myself, to trust the process."

Sahil's voice filled with pride. "Exactly. You've come too far to let go of what makes your consultancy special. Stay true to your instincts and your vision. The rest will fall into place."

They spoke for a while longer, laughter and memories softening the conversation. By the time they hung up, Aniket felt lighter, as though the fog of doubt had lifted, leaving clarity in its place.

He walked over to the whiteboard in his office, where a detailed list of potential clients, financial targets, and strategic goals had been written out over the past few months. Without hesitation, he reached for the eraser and wiped the board clean. The act felt symbolic—a cleansing of the distractions and the doubts, a return to the core of why he had started this journey in the first place.

He picked up a marker and, in bold letters, wrote a single word at the top of the board: **Vision.**

That was the key—his vision, his passion for helping businesses grow, for supporting a diverse range of clients. That was what mattered most, not the security of one large contract, not the fleeting comfort of stability.

Aniket sat back down at his desk, his mind clear, his heart steady. With renewed determination, he composed an email to Mr. Verma, his fingers moving with purpose over the keyboard.

Dear Mr. Verma,

Thank you for your generous offer. After careful consideration, I've decided to decline the long-term contract. While I value our partnership and look forward to working together, I need to stay true to the mission and vision of my consultancy, which is to support a diverse range of clients and projects.

I appreciate your understanding and am excited to continue our collaboration in a way that aligns with both our values.

Sincerely, Aniket Sharma

He hit send, a wave of relief washing over him. He had made the right choice—the choice that stayed true to his values, his purpose.

Because sometimes, the greatest success didn't lie in security or stability, but in the courage to remain true to yourself, your vision, and the dreams that had driven you from the very beginning.

Aniket knew now that while success could feel like freedom, it could also become a set of chains if not aligned with purpose. And he had just broken free.

CHAPTER THIRTY-FIVE

The Freedom to Fail

Aniket sat at his desk, staring at the latest email on his laptop screen. It was a polite but firm rejection of the proposal he had poured weeks of effort into. The disappointment was undeniable, settling like a dull ache in his chest, but it wasn't the overwhelming sting it had once been. This time, it felt different—softer, almost reflective. He wasn't crushed by it. He had learned to accept it.

He leaned back, letting his fingers tap lightly on the wooden surface of his desk as his thoughts wandered back to the decision he'd made a few weeks ago. Turning down the long-term contract with Mr. Verma's corporation had been a pivotal moment for him, a choice that favoured vision over security. At the time, it had felt right—an alignment with the core of who he was and what he wanted his consultancy to stand for. But now, faced with another rejection, he wondered: Had he made the right choice? Was he being too idealistic? Too stubborn?

He glanced at the whiteboard in his office, where "Vision" was still written boldly across the top. Beneath it, however, were the telltale signs of struggle—projects crossed out, ideas abandoned, and a collection of failed attempts. Each one was a reminder of the risks he'd taken and the setbacks he'd faced, but they were also evidence of his resilience, his refusal to play it safe.

Aniket took a deep breath. He had made his peace with failure as a concept, but every rejection still left room for doubt. And today, the doubt was creeping in. Maybe, just maybe, he was missing something. Maybe he was too focused on maintaining his ideals. What if, by refusing the safe path, he was condemning himself to a series of struggles?

Before his thoughts could spiral any further, he reached for his phone and instinctively dialled Sahil's number. The phone rang twice before his friend answered with his usual warmth.

"Aniket! What's going on? You sound like you've been carrying the weight of the world again."

Aniket smiled faintly, the sound of Sahil's voice already easing some of the tension. "I got another rejection today, Sahil. Another proposal that didn't make the cut. And, well, I'm starting to wonder if I'm just banging my head against the wall. Maybe I'm missing something."

Sahil paused for a moment before responding, his voice thoughtful. "Rejection stings. I won't lie to you about that. But you're not missing anything, Aniket. The thing is, when you put yourself out there—when you take risks—failure is part of the deal. It's not something you can avoid, but something you can learn from. Failure is often more valuable than success, even though it doesn't feel that way at first."

Aniket leaned back, looking at the ceiling, his mind heavy with doubts. "I know you're right, Sahil. But it's hard to keep going when it feels like all you're doing is failing."

Sahil chuckled softly; the sound rich with understanding. "I know the feeling. There were times I wanted to throw in the towel, times when I thought I wasn't cut out for this. But here's what I've learned—failure isn't a reflection of who we are. It's just part of the process. It's a sign that you're pushing boundaries, that you're trying something new. You're doing meaningful work, Aniket. That's what matters."

Aniket felt a wave of gratitude wash over him. Sahil always had a way of putting things in perspective, reminding him why he started down this path. "I know you're right," he said quietly. "I just needed to hear it again."

"You're building something that's going to last, Aniket," Sahil continued, his tone firm but encouraging. "You're taking risks, and you're going to face setbacks. But that's what makes the success all the more meaningful when it comes. It's not just about the wins—it's about having the courage to fail, and the strength to keep going after you do."

They talked for a while longer, their conversation a blend of support, humour, and memories. When they finally hung up, Aniket felt lighter. The conversation had lifted the weight he had been carrying, allowing him to breathe more easily.

He stood up and walked over to the whiteboard. He looked at the crossed-out projects and the failed attempts, but instead of seeing defeat, he saw evidence of his growth. Each failure had taught him something, had brought him closer to the next breakthrough. Sahil was right—failure wasn't the end. It was part of the journey.

Picking up a marker, he wrote out a new idea at the bottom of the board. It was something that had been brewing in the back of his mind for weeks but had never made its way to the surface until now.

The new project had the potential to fail like the others before it, but that didn't bother him anymore. He had learned that failure wasn't something to fear—it was something to embrace. With each attempt, whether successful or not, he was moving forward, growing, and discovering new possibilities.

Aniket returned to his desk, his mind buzzing with excitement as he sketched out the first details of the project. There would be challenges, he knew that. There would be setbacks and more failures, but he was ready for them. He was ready to create, to innovate, and to take the risks that came with building something meaningful.

Because, sometimes, the real success wasn't in avoiding failure—it was in finding the courage to keep going, no matter what.

Across the city, Sahil stood in front of a large audience in a brightly lit auditorium. The room was filled with young entrepreneurs, their faces alight with hope and anticipation. They had come to hear Sahil speak about his journey—about the successes that had made him a household name, but more importantly, about the failures that had shaped his path.

He looked out over the crowd, feeling a sense of responsibility as he began to speak. "Thank you all for being here today. I'm honoured to share my story with you, but more than that, I want to talk to you about something we don't hear enough about: failure."

There was a ripple of interest, the room growing quieter as his words sank in. Sahil smiled softly, recognizing the eagerness in their eyes, the same eagerness he had once carried in his heart.

"Failure," he continued, "is something you're all going to face, probably more times than you'd like. It's going to hurt. It's going to make you question everything. But here's the thing—failure is not the opposite of success. It's a part of it."

A young woman in the front row raised her hand. "Sahil Sir, how do you keep going when everything seems to be falling apart? How do you deal with failure?"

Sahil smiled warmly at her. "That's a great question. For me, it's all about perspective. When something doesn't go the way I hoped, it's easy to feel like I've failed. But when you step back, you realize that each setback is just one moment in a much larger journey. Success isn't about avoiding failure—it's about resilience, about getting back up and trying again."

He paused, letting the words sink in before continuing. "Failure isn't a sign that you're not good enough. It's proof that you're pushing yourself beyond your comfort zone. It's proof that you're trying something new, something challenging. And that's how you grow."

There were more nods of agreement, and Sahil could see the realization dawn on many of their faces. Failure wasn't the enemy they had been taught to fear—it was a teacher, a guide, something to learn from.

"But there's another aspect to failure," Sahil added. "It's about challenging the way society defines success. We're often told that success is about reaching a specific goal, about avoiding mistakes. But that's not true. Success is about the journey, about learning, and about being brave enough to take risks."

Another young man raised his hand. "How do you redefine success in a world that focuses so much on the end result?"

Sahil nodded thoughtfully. "It's about shifting your mindset. Instead of seeing success as the destination, see it as the process—the growth, the lessons learned, the courage to keep moving forward. True success isn't about avoiding failure; it's about how you handle it, how you use it to fuel your next step."

As the session continued, the questions flowed, and Sahil could feel the energy in the room shift. The conversation deepened, touching on resilience, creativity, and the importance of purpose. By the end of the evening, Sahil knew that they had built something real—a shared understanding that failure was not something to be feared, but something to be embraced.

Later that night, Aniket sat back at his desk, feeling a sense of peace that went beyond the day's events. The words he had written on the whiteboard felt more significant now: **"Embrace failure, build the future."**

He smiled as he added another line beneath it: **"One step, one failure, one success at a time."**

This was his journey—one built not just on success, but on the courage to fail, to grow, and to keep building, no matter the outcome.

Because sometimes, the freedom to fail was the key to building something truly extraordinary.

CHAPTER THIRTY-SIX

The Ripple Effect

Aniket sat in the quiet of his office, the soft glow from the desk lamp casting a warm light across the room. He scrolled through his emails, his attention caught by a message from an old colleague he hadn't spoken to in years. The words on the screen carried an unexpected weight that touched him deeply:

"Aniket, I've been following your journey from a distance, and I just wanted to say how much your story has inspired me. I've been stuck in a corporate job for the past ten years, always too afraid to take the leap into starting my own business. But seeing what you've built, the risks you've taken, the failures you've embraced—it's given me the courage to finally take that step. Thank you for showing me that it's okay to fail, that it's okay to dream."

Aniket leaned back in his chair, letting the words sink in. His heart swelled with a mix of pride and humility. It was surreal to think that his struggles, the ups and downs of his journey, had touched someone else's life in such a profound way. When he had started out, the path had felt so personal—just him, carving out a meaningful career. But now, the realization that his story had become a source of inspiration for others was both humbling and exhilarating.

His eyes flicked over to the whiteboard across the room, where the words "Embrace failure, build the future" were written in bold. That phrase had become a mantra for him, guiding him through every setback, every moment of doubt. And now, it seemed those ripples were spreading beyond his own life, affecting others in ways he hadn't anticipated.

The door to his office creaked open, and Meera, his assistant, stepped in, her face lit up with excitement. "Aniket, there's someone here to see you. He says he's an old friend."

Aniket raised an eyebrow, curiosity piqued. "An old friend? Who is it?"

Before Meera could respond, a familiar face appeared in the doorway. It was Rajat, a former classmate, someone he hadn't seen in years. Rajat's smile was wide, his eyes bright with excitement.

"Aniket! It's been too long," Rajat said, striding into the room and pulling Aniket into a tight hug.

Aniket laughed, surprised but genuinely happy to see him. "Rajat! What brings you here? I haven't heard from you in ages."

Rajat stepped back, his smile fading slightly, replaced by a more serious expression. "I've been following your journey, Aniket. Watching what you've built, the risks you've taken—it's been eye-opening."

Aniket gestured toward the chair in front of his desk, his curiosity deepening. "What do you mean?"

Rajat sat down, clasping his hands together as he spoke. "I've been stuck in the same corporate job for a decade now. It pays well, but it doesn't fulfil me. For years, I've dreamed of starting my own business, but I've always been too afraid to take the leap."

He paused, looking Aniket directly in the eyes. "But seeing what you've done—leaving behind security, facing failure head-on—it made me realize that I don't have to stay trapped. If you could take the risks and follow your passion, why can't I?"

Aniket felt a lump form in his throat. He wasn't used to hearing this kind of praise, especially from someone he'd always seen as an equal. "Rajat, I don't know what to say. I never thought my journey would have that kind of impact on anyone."

Rajat's expression softened, and he leaned forward slightly. "You've shown me that it's okay to fail, that it's okay to take risks and follow your heart. That's why I'm here today. I've decided to quit my job and start my own venture. I wanted to tell you in person—and to thank you for inspiring me."

Tears pricked at the corners of Aniket's eyes. The weight of Rajat's words settled over him, heavy and humbling. "I don't know if I deserve that, Rajat. I've just been trying to figure things out, trying to build something that matters to me."

Rajat smiled, his hand reaching across the desk to grip Aniket's. "You've done more than that, my friend. You've created a ripple. You're touching more lives than you know."

For a moment, they sat in silence, both reflecting on the depth of what had just been said. Aniket felt an overwhelming sense of awe and responsibility. What had begun as a personal journey now seemed much larger, a story that was encouraging others to pursue their own paths, to take their own risks.

They spent the next hour talking, sharing dreams and fears, much like they had years ago in the early days of their careers. Rajat's excitement was infectious, his plans for his new business bold and ambitious. Aniket felt a renewed sense of energy and purpose as he listened and offered advice, seeing the fire in Rajat's eyes.

When Rajat finally left, his face glowing with hope, Aniket sat back at his desk, his heart full. He picked up his phone, his fingers moving almost instinctively as he typed out a message to Sahil.

"Rajat just left my office. He's starting his own business; says he was inspired by my journey. It's amazing, Sahil. The ripple is spreading."

He hit send, a smile tugging at his lips as he leaned back in his chair. His mind buzzed with thoughts of the future; of the unexpected impact his choices were having on the people around him.

Meanwhile, across the country, Sahil stood in front of a packed lecture hall, feeling that familiar mix of excitement and anticipation. The room was filled with business students, their eyes bright with curiosity as they waited for him to speak.

He had been invited to give a guest lecture at one of the top business schools, a chance to share his journey with the next generation of entrepreneurs. It was a surreal experience, standing before these eager faces, knowing that his failures and successes were now case studies in resilience, innovation, and the power of embracing risk.

Sahil took a deep breath, his heart swelling with a sense of responsibility and purpose. "Thank you all for being here today," he began, his voice steady. "I'm honoured to have the opportunity to share my journey, to talk about the lessons I've learned—the successes, the failures, and everything in between."

A murmur of excitement rippled through the room as Sahil began his story, starting with the early days—when everything was uncertain, and every decision felt like a gamble. The sleepless nights filled with doubt, the moments when it felt like the world was falling apart, and the failures that had nearly derailed him.

"But here's what I learned," Sahil continued, his voice growing stronger. "Failure isn't the end. It's a part of the process, a stepping stone on the path to success. It's something to embrace, not fear."

He looked out at the faces of the students, remembering how, not long ago, he had been in their place—unsure, but eager, dreaming of a future filled with possibilities. "You're all going to face challenges," he said, his tone soft but firm. "You're going to fail, probably more than once. But that's okay. Because it's not the failure that defines you. It's how you respond to it—how you learn, how you grow."

Hands began to shoot up across the room, questions flowing in rapid succession. The discussion deepened, touching on resilience, creativity, and the importance of staying true to your purpose even in the face of adversity.

"Mr. Sahil," a young woman in the front row asked, "what's the most important lesson for someone who's just starting out?"

Sahil paused, considering the question carefully. "The most important lesson is to stay true to yourself," he said. "To your vision, to your values. The world will try to pull you in different directions, but if you can stay grounded in why you started, you'll find the strength to keep going, no matter what."

Nods of understanding rippled through the room, and Sahil felt a deep sense of connection with these young dreamers. They were ready to take on the world, just as he had once been, and now, he was in a position to guide them on their own journeys.

Later that evening, back in his office, Aniket felt a surge of inspiration. He looked at the whiteboard, where the words of his latest project were written boldly—a reminder of the journey he had taken, the risks he had faced, and the person he was becoming.

He picked up the marker, writing a few more words beneath it:

"Inspire, build, create."

He stepped back, feeling a renewed sense of purpose. The ripples of his journey were spreading, touching more lives than he could have imagined. And as he stood there, his heart filled with hope and determination, he knew he was ready to continue building, to continue inspiring.

Because sometimes, the greatest impact wasn't in the successes you achieved for yourself, but in the way your journey inspired others to take their own first steps.

CHAPTER THIRTY-SEVEN

The Fallacy of Perfection

Aniket sat in his office, the city's hum faintly audible through the large windows as he gazed at the framed certificates that lined the wall. They had once symbolized everything he aspired to—excellence, achievement, perfection. Each certificate was a reminder of his relentless pursuit to be the best, to never make a mistake, to always stay on top. He had taken immense pride in them, believing they defined who he was and the path to success. But now, as he stared at them, a strange sense of detachment settled in.

What had once felt like milestones now seemed like artifacts from another life—one that had been driven by the need to be perfect, to avoid failure at all costs. Aniket slowly stood up, walking toward the wall. His fingers lightly brushed over the glass of one of the frames as memories flooded back—long nights spent studying, the anxiety of tests, and the constant pressure to maintain a flawless record. He had been taught that perfection was the key to success, and for a long time, he had believed it.

He turned away, letting out a sigh as he walked back to his desk. His eyes landed on the whiteboard, where the words *"Embrace failure, build the future"* were boldly written. It had taken him years to truly understand that failure wasn't something to fear but something to learn from. The pursuit of perfection had trapped him, narrowed his vision, and kept him from appreciating the beauty of growth through mistakes.

Aniket sat down, the weight of his realization heavy in his chest. He had spent so much of his life chasing after an ideal that didn't exist. The perfect grades, the perfect career, the perfect life—all of it had come at a cost. He had been so focused on achieving stability and security that he had forgotten to enjoy the journey. Now, it felt clear that true growth didn't come from avoiding failure but from embracing it, from taking risks and making mistakes.

He picked up his phone, feeling the need to talk to someone who would understand. His fingers hovered over the screen before he dialled Sahil's number. The phone rang twice before Sahil's familiar voice greeted him.

"Aniket! It's always good to hear from you. How's everything going?"

Aniket smiled, though there was a heaviness in his heart. "I've been thinking a lot, Sahil. About perfection, success, and what it all means. I think I've spent too long chasing something that doesn't really matter."

There was a pause on the line before Sahil's voice came through, calm and thoughtful. "What do you mean?"

Aniket leaned back in his chair, staring at the certificates on the wall. "I've been reflecting on my life—on how much time I spent trying to be perfect. The perfect grades, the perfect job, the perfect path. But looking back, I wonder if it was all an illusion. I was chasing something that wasn't real, wasn't fulfilling."

Sahil sighed; his voice filled with understanding. "I get it, Aniket. We're conditioned to believe that perfection is the goal, that success is about avoiding mistakes and staying in control. But the truth is, perfection is a myth. It keeps us from taking risks, from learning, from living fully."

Aniket nodded, the realization settling in deeper. "Exactly. I've spent so much time trying to avoid failure, trying to control every outcome. But now I see that the moments I grew the most were the moments when I stumbled, when I faced setbacks. But that's not what we're taught, is it? We're taught to fear failure, to avoid it at all costs."

Sahil's voice softened, filled with reassurance. "You're right, Aniket. Our entire education system, and society for that matter, is built on the idea that failure is something to be ashamed of. We're judged by grades, titles, and achievements, and we internalize that as the only measure of success. But in the real world, success comes from resilience, from creativity, from being willing to fail."

Aniket felt a surge of frustration. "So how do we change that? How do we break free from this mindset and teach people that failure isn't something to be feared, but something to embrace?"

Sahil's voice was firm with resolve. "It starts with us. People like you and me who've experienced failure and come out stronger. We need to share our stories, challenge the narrative, and redefine what success really means. We need to show that it's okay to be imperfect, to make mistakes, to learn as we go."

A sense of hope stirred in Aniket, lightening the weight that had been pressing down on him. "You're right, Sahil. We need to change the conversation. We need to show that it's not about achieving perfection, but about growth, about resilience, about being courageous enough to keep going."

They talked for a while longer, reflecting on their journeys and the lessons they had learned along the way. By the time they hung up, Aniket felt a clarity he hadn't felt in a long time.

He turned to his desk, his mind buzzing with thoughts. The fallacy of perfection had kept him chained for too long, but now, he saw it for what it was—an illusion. He picked up his pen and began writing, pouring out his thoughts onto the page, determined to share his story, to show others that it was okay to be imperfect, to take risks, to fail, and to grow.

Meanwhile, in a grand conference hall filled with the hum of anticipation, Sahil stood at a podium, his heart racing with excitement. The room was packed with educators, policymakers, and business leaders, all gathered to hear him speak at a global conference on education and innovation. The topic was one he was deeply passionate about—the need for an education system that embraced failure as a learning tool rather than something to be feared.

He took a deep breath, scanning the room. These were the people who could help shape the future, who could influence how society viewed failure and success. "Thank you all for being here today," he began, his voice steady. "It's an honour to speak with you about something that has profoundly shaped my life—the fallacy of perfection and the need for a more practical, failure-embracing education system."

A murmur of agreement rippled through the audience, and Sahil felt a surge of gratitude. He had the chance to share something that could change lives, just as failure had changed his own.

"I want to start with a story," Sahil continued, his voice calm yet firm. "A story about a young man who grew up in a education system which taught us that perfection was the key to success. He was taught that his worth was measured by grades, by achievements, by how flawless his life appeared. For years, he chased that illusion—afraid of making mistakes, afraid of failure."

He paused, letting the weight of his words settle over the room. "But eventually, he realized something: perfection was a lie. The real growth, the real learning, came not from being perfect, but from facing challenges, making mistakes, and learning from failure."

Sahil's gaze swept the room, taking in the thoughtful expressions of the audience. "That young man was me. I spent initial years chasing perfection, afraid to fail. But very soon I defied this education system and started doing what I truly believe and what I am good at. When I learned to take risks, I found true success—not the kind measured by grades or titles, but the kind measured by growth and purpose."

A silence fell over the room as his words resonated with the audience. Slowly, hands began to rise, and the conversation deepened. The questions were thoughtful, probing the very foundation of what society had taught them about success and failure.

"How do we change the system?" one woman asked, her voice filled with urgency. "How do we teach our students that it's okay to fail, to take risks?"

Sahil nodded; his passion clear. "We need to redefine success. We need to move away from a system that values grades and test scores above all else. Instead, we should focus on creativity, resilience, and the ability to learn from failure. We need to create an environment where students feel safe to experiment, to make mistakes, and to grow."

As the conversation continued, Sahil felt the room come alive with possibilities. This wasn't just a lecture—it was the beginning of a movement. A shift in how they thought about education, about growth, about life itself.

Later that evening, as Aniket sat in his office, he reflected on his conversation with Sahil. He glanced at the whiteboard, where the bold letters reminded him of the journey he was on.

He picked up the marker, adding a few more words beneath the phrase. *"Embrace the imperfect, build the future."*

Stepping back, Aniket smiled. He was ready for whatever came next, knowing that it wasn't perfection he was striving for—it was growth. One mistake, one failure, one step at a time.

CHAPTER THIRTY-EIGHT

The Call for Change

Aniket stood amidst the crowded auditorium, his heart thudding in his chest as he surveyed the room. Educators, parents, students, and activists filled the space, united by a shared belief in a common goal: to transform the education system. The air buzzed with the energy of people who knew change was not just necessary, but inevitable. They were gathered to discuss a new kind of education—one that didn't just push students toward success but taught them to embrace failure, to learn from it, and to grow stronger because of it.

Aniket's gaze flicked to the stage, where a panel of speakers sat, each representing different aspects of the movement for educational reform. His eyes lingered on Sahil, who was seated confidently at the center of the table. A sense of pride welled up inside Aniket. Sahil had become a symbol of resilience, of breaking free from conventional paths and creating meaningful change. Now, here they were, part of a growing movement challenging the old ways and demanding a more humane, practical education system.

The moderator's voice broke through Aniket's thoughts. "Welcome, everyone, and thank you for joining us for this important conversation. Today, we're here to discuss the future of education—how we can create a system that not only measures success by grades but by resilience, creativity, and the ability to thrive in an ever-changing world."

Applause filled the room, but Aniket's heart pounded for what came next. Sahil was about to speak, and it felt as if the entire room was holding its breath. The moderator continued; her voice filled with admiration. "It's an honour to introduce Sahil Patel, a visionary entrepreneur who has been working closely with educators to design a curriculum that balances theory with practice, preparing students for the real challenges ahead."

Sahil stood up, his presence calm yet commanding. The applause that greeted him was thunderous, but Sahil waited for it to subside before he began. His voice was steady, filled with conviction as he addressed the audience. "We are standing at a critical juncture in history, one where we have the opportunity to rethink education—not just what we teach, but how we teach it."

He paused for a moment, letting his words sink in. "For too long, we've focused on test scores, memorization, and rigid success metrics. But that's not what our children need to thrive in a world that's rapidly evolving. They need to learn to think critically, to solve problems, to innovate. Most importantly, they need to understand that failure is not something to fear but something to embrace. It is through failure that we learn, that we grow, and that we develop the resilience to face whatever challenges come our way."

The murmur of agreement from the crowd was almost palpable. Aniket, seated in the back, felt the surge of hope that spread through the room. Sahil's words weren't just inspirational—they were a call to action.

"We are working on a curriculum that doesn't just focus on what students should know, but on who they need to become," Sahil continued. "A curriculum that values creativity, that fosters curiosity, and that teaches our children to face the world's uncertainties with confidence and adaptability."

Another round of applause broke out, but this time, it was quieter—more thoughtful, more reflective. Sahil leaned back in his chair, and his eyes met Aniket's across the room. In that moment, there was a shared understanding between them—an acknowledgment of the journey they had both been on, and of the work that still lay ahead.

The discussion continued with the other panellists weighing in, offering their own insights and visions for the future of education. Each speaker built upon the last, weaving a tapestry of ideas that made it clear—change was not just possible, it was happening.

As the session drew to a close, the moderator spoke again, her voice tinged with excitement. "We have time for one last question. Aniket Sharma, I believe you had something to share?"

Aniket's heart skipped a beat. He hadn't expected to be called on. Slowly, he rose from his seat, feeling the weight of the moment settle over him. He glanced around the room, all eyes now on him, and took a steadying breath.

"Thank you," he began, his voice steady despite the flutter of nerves. "It's an honour to be here, to be part of this conversation. I've been on my own journey—one that's taught me the importance of failure, the value of resilience, and the need for a more practical, more compassionate education system."

His gaze drifted to Sahil as he continued. "I've been deeply inspired by the work Sahil and so many others are doing to challenge the status quo and push for real change. It's given me the courage to believe that we can create an education system that values growth over perfection, that prepares our children not just to survive, but to thrive in an unpredictable world."

The room erupted in applause, and Aniket felt a wave of emotion wash over him. He sat down, his heart lighter than it had been in a long time. He was ready—ready to be part of this movement, ready to make a difference.

Later that evening, the sun had dipped below the horizon, casting the city in twilight. Inside a small meeting room, the energy was still buzzing. Aniket sat at the table with a group of educators, activists, and parents. Sahil sat at the head, calmly outlining the next steps in their plan.

"We need to start small," Sahil said, his voice steady and focused. "We can't overhaul the entire system overnight. But we can pilot the curriculum in a few schools that are willing to innovate. We'll gather feedback, refine the process, and build a network of like-minded educators and institutions who believe in this vision."

Heads nodded around the table, and murmurs of agreement spread. The enthusiasm in the room was infectious, and Aniket could feel the momentum building. The challenges ahead were daunting, but the determination in the room was undeniable.

"We're not just building a curriculum," Sahil continued, his voice gaining intensity. "We're building a movement. A movement that redefines success, that teaches resilience, that values creativity and human potential. This is about more than education—this is about the future we want to create."

The room fell silent for a moment as Sahil's words hung in the air. Then, one by one, people began to nod. They were ready. They believed in this mission, in this call for change. They understood that the road ahead would be difficult, but they were willing to fight for it.

Aniket's chest swelled with pride. This was it. This was the reason he had pushed himself, the reason he had embraced failure, taken risks, and refused to give up. He wasn't just building a business—he was building a future.

He glanced at Sahil, who met his gaze with a knowing smile. There was no need for words between them. They both understood the significance of this moment, of what they were working to achieve.

Aniket picked up his phone and, with a renewed sense of purpose, began jotting down ideas for how he could help implement the curriculum. This wasn't just about education reform—it was about changing the way people thought about success and failure, about giving future generations the tools they needed to navigate a complex and unpredictable world.

As the meeting wrapped up, Aniket walked out into the night, the cool air a welcome contrast to the charged energy inside. He felt alive with possibility, with the certainty that they were on the brink of something monumental. This wasn't just a project—it was a movement, and he was ready to be at the forefront.

Because this was more than just business. It was about creating a future where people were free to fail, to grow, and to succeed on their own terms. A future where education prepared children not just for exams, but for life.

And Aniket knew, with absolute clarity, that this was a future worth fighting for.

CHAPTER THIRTY-NINE

The Meeting

The sun dipped lower in the sky, casting a warm, golden hue across the bustling city as Aniket made his way to the small café nestled at the corner of a quieter street. This café, with its large windows overlooking a peaceful garden, was a sanctuary from the noise and rush of urban life. Today, it was the perfect place for a long-overdue reunion.

It had been nearly a year since Aniket had last seen Sahil in person. While they had kept in touch through phone calls and occasional video chats, the hectic pace of their respective lives had kept them apart. But as Aniket walked through the door and spotted Sahil sitting at a table in the corner, the memories of their friendship and shared history surged forward, bringing a warm smile to his face.

Sahil looked up, his expression lighting up with joy as he stood to greet Aniket. "Aniket! It's so good to see you, my friend," he said, extending his hand.

Aniket clasped it, the familiar grip of Sahil's handshake instantly grounding him. They embraced briefly, the years and distance between them melting away. "Too long, Sahil," Aniket replied with a chuckle. "You look great."

Sahil laughed, his eyes twinkling with the same humour Aniket remembered from their youth. "I've been surviving," he said, motioning for Aniket to sit. "And you? You look like a man on a mission."

Aniket smiled as he sat down, the weight of the last few months lifting slightly. "I suppose I am. But then, aren't we all? I've been keeping an eye on your work—what you've done with the education reform is amazing, Sahil."

Sahil waved the compliment away with a modest smile. "It's been a tough road, but we're moving forward. I've heard great things about you, too. You've been working with schools, pushing for change. You've really become part of the movement."

Aniket nodded, feeling a sense of pride welling up inside him. "I never thought I'd be here, doing this. I always imagined myself in business, focused on growth and success. But there's more to life than profit margins. You were right, Sahil—it's about creating something that matters, something that gives back."

Sahil's expression grew serious, reflective. "We've both come a long way, haven't we? From chasing grades and striving for perfection to this." He gestured around them, his voice filled with quiet pride. "We've found our paths. That's what success is, Aniket. It's not about reaching a destination or achieving a perfect life. It's about the journey, the growth, and the impact we have along the way."

Aniket felt a lump form in his throat as he absorbed Sahil's words. "You've always known that, Sahil. Even when we were younger, you had the clarity and courage to follow your own path."

Sahil shook his head slightly, his smile turning wistful. "I've had my doubts, just like anyone else. But I've learned it's okay to be afraid. It's okay to fail. That's where the real growth happens."

A moment of silence fell between them as they reflected on the struggles, triumphs, and lessons they had learned over the years. Then, the conversation picked up again, flowing naturally, as they shared the stories of their respective journeys.

Aniket told Sahil about his decision to join the education reform movement, along with his thriving consultancy. He spoke of the uncertainty and fear that had accompanied that choice—the doubt that sometimes crept in as he wondered if he had made the right decision.

"There were days when I thought I'd made the biggest mistake of my life," Aniket admitted, his voice soft. "I'd built something successful, something stable, and I walked away from it to dive into the unknown. I didn't know if I was making a difference or just throwing away everything I'd worked for."

Sahil listened intently, his expression one of deep understanding. "I know that feeling all too well," he said. "Every time we hit resistance, every time progress seemed slow, I'd wonder if we were really making a difference. But I'd remind myself why we started—why we couldn't settle for the way things were."

Aniket nodded, feeling reassured by Sahil's words. "It's funny," he said, smiling. "When I think about what you've accomplished, Sahil, it's clear you've made a huge impact. You've inspired people, built something that's changing lives."

Sahil smiled back; his tone humble. "And so have you. You've inspired others to take risks, to believe in themselves, and to challenge the system. That's no small thing, Aniket."

They sat in comfortable silence for a moment, the quiet hum of the café surrounding them. Then, Aniket broke the stillness with a question that had been lingering in his mind.

"Do you ever wonder what would've happened if we hadn't taken those risks? If we had just stayed on the path we were on, chasing stability and perfection?"

Sahil leaned back in his chair; his expression thoughtful. "Sometimes," he said. "But then I remember that the reason we've been able to do what we've done is because we took those risks. We were willing to step into uncertainty, to fail, and to learn. Without that, we wouldn't have found our paths or made the impact we've made."

Aniket felt a wave of gratitude wash over him. "You're right," he said quietly. "We've both been successful in our own ways. And I think that's what matters—not the money, not the titles, but the lives we've touched and the change we've made."

Sahil's eyes shone with pride as he nodded in agreement. "We've come full circle, haven't we? From those days of chasing grades and fearing failure, to this—two friends, sitting in a café, talking about life, success, and the journey we've been on."

Aniket laughed, feeling a sense of liberation in the simplicity of the moment. "It's amazing how far we've come. And yet, in some ways, we're still the same—still searching, still learning."

Sahil leaned forward, his voice filled with warmth. "That's the beauty of it, Aniket. We're always growing, always evolving. And that's what makes life meaningful—the journey, the learning, and the people we meet along the way."

They sat quietly for a while, both lost in thought, reflecting on the years that had passed and the lessons they had learned. It was a moment heavy with the significance of their shared history and the bond that had only grown stronger with time.

As the conversation moved forward, they began to talk about the future—about the work they were doing, the schools they were helping, and the dreams they still held. They spoke of the curriculum Sahil was building, and how it was inspiring educators to think differently about teaching and learning. Aniket shared stories of the schools he had been working with, how teachers and students alike were embracing the idea of resilience and growth through failure.

They talked late into the evening, the café slowly emptying around them as the city outside quieted into the calm of the night. Aniket felt a deep sense of fulfilment as they spoke—not just because of what they had accomplished, but because of the possibility of what was still to come.

As they stood to leave, the weight of the years lifted from their shoulders, replaced by the excitement of the future. Aniket felt lighter, more certain than ever that they were on the right path, and that their work—together and individually—was just beginning.

"I'm glad we did this," Aniket said as they stepped out into the cool night air. "It's easy to get caught up in the day-to-day, but nights like this remind me of why we're doing what we're doing."

Sahil nodded, his smile filled with warmth and understanding. "It's not always easy, but it's worth it. And we've got each other to keep us going."

They clasped hands once more, a gesture of friendship and mutual respect, before parting ways. As Aniket walked down the quiet street, the city lights twinkling above, he knew this was only the beginning. There were still many paths to explore, many lessons to learn, and many lives to touch. But he was ready—for the challenges, the risks, the failures, and the growth that would come with it all.

Because for Aniket, success was no longer about reaching a destination. It was about the journey, the people, and the impact he would make along the way. And that, he knew, was a path worth walking.

CHAPTER FORTY

A New Dawn

The sun rose slowly over the city, casting a soft, golden light that illuminated everything in its path with a quiet promise of new beginnings. Aniket stood on the balcony of his apartment, the cool morning air brushing against his face as he gazed at the skyline. A sense of peace and clarity filled him—today was the start of a new chapter in his life, one that held endless possibilities. But this wasn't about chasing after success as he once knew it. Today, he was stepping forward not as a struggling entrepreneur or someone searching for his place, but as a partner, a collaborator, someone committed to building something meaningful alongside his friend Sahil.

In the days leading up to this moment, Aniket had done a lot of reflecting. Sahil had offered him something powerful—a partnership not just in business, but in purpose. It wasn't an easy decision; it had required him to set aside his pride, confront his insecurities, and embrace the idea of change. But now, standing on his balcony, watching the first light of the day break across the horizon, he knew in his heart that he had made the right choice. There was a deep calm within him, a renewed sense of purpose.

Turning away from the view, Aniket walked back into his apartment, his steps light with determination. The partnership agreement lay neatly on the table—a symbol of trust and belief, not just from Sahil but from himself. He had spent days going over every detail, every clause, considering the future they were about to build. With a steady hand, he picked up the pen and signed his name at the bottom, sealing his commitment to this new venture. It was the culmination of a journey that had begun long ago, rooted in a friendship that had grown into something extraordinary.

Taking a deep breath, Aniket felt the familiar flutter of excitement mingling with resolve. This was it. The moment that would define the next chapter of his life. He picked up his phone and dialled Sahil's number, the familiar rhythm of the ringing filling the quiet room.

"Aniket!" came Sahil's voice, warm and filled with excitement. "I've been waiting to hear from you. Did you sign the papers?"

Aniket smiled, glancing at the signed document. "I did, Sahil. I'm all in. Let's build something incredible together."

There was a brief silence before Sahil's voice returned, filled with joy and anticipation. "That's fantastic, Aniket! I can't tell you how happy I am. This is going to be amazing. We're going to change the world, my friend. I know it."

Aniket felt a surge of excitement as the words settled in, the reality of what they were about to do taking shape in his mind. "I'm excited too, Sahil. I know it won't be easy, but I believe in this—what we're building, what we're going to accomplish together."

Sahil laughed; his voice contagious with optimism. "We've faced tougher challenges before. This is just the beginning. We're going to break barriers, redefine what success really means, and create something that will last for generations."

Aniket nodded, his heart swelling with a deep sense of purpose. "I've been thinking a lot about that lately. Success isn't just about money or status. It's about impact, about building something that outlives us and changes lives."

Sahil's tone softened, reflecting the depth of their shared mission. "Exactly, Aniket. Too many people get caught up in chasing stability, in avoiding failure. But we have the chance to show them a different way. We're going to create something that empowers people to take risks, to embrace growth, and to reimagine success."

As Aniket listened to Sahil, he felt a deep pride in the journey they were about to embark on. "And we're going to do it. We're going to show that success is a process—about evolving, about becoming. It's not a destination."

The conversation flowed from there, filled with plans, ideas, and dreams about what they could achieve together. By the time they hung up, Aniket felt a sense of determination he hadn't felt in years. This was more than just business. This was about creating a legacy, a future that mattered.

The following weeks passed in a whirlwind of activity. Aniket and Sahil threw themselves into the work of building their new venture—meeting with educators, business leaders, and innovators to gather insights and form partnerships. Their mission was clear: to build something revolutionary, something that would challenge the old ways of thinking about success and failure.

They worked tirelessly, often staying up late into the night, their conversations filled with excitement and possibility. Each decision felt monumental, each step forward a significant one. But the journey wasn't without its setbacks. They faced resistance, doubt from others, and their own moments of frustration. But through it all, Aniket felt something he hadn't experienced in a long time—an unshakable belief that they were on the right path.

Sahil's presence was a steadying force. His vision, his unwavering commitment to their shared mission, kept them grounded. He reminded Aniket of why they had taken on this challenge in the first place—because they wanted to make a difference.

One evening, as they sat together in Sahil's office, pouring over the final details of their new initiative, Aniket couldn't help but reflect on how far they had come.

"You know, Sahil," he said, his voice soft with emotion, "I never imagined we'd be here. Doing this. Building something like this. It's incredible."

Sahil looked up from the papers, his expression thoughtful but filled with warmth. "We have come a long way, haven't we? But this is just the beginning, Aniket. There's still so much more we can do—so many lives we can touch, so much change we can make."

Aniket nodded, feeling the truth of Sahil's words resonate deep within him. "And we will. We're going to build something that changes the way people think about life, about success. We're going to show them that it's okay to take risks, that growth comes from failure and from embracing the journey."

Sahil leaned back in his chair, his eyes filled with pride and hope. "Everything we've been through—the struggles, the doubts—it's brought us here. This is where we were meant to be, Aniket."

They sat in silence for a moment, both absorbing the enormity of what they were about to accomplish. Then, slowly, they began to speak again—about the future, about the challenges that still lay ahead, about the vision they were committed to bringing to life.

The day of the launch finally arrived. The spacious hall where the event was being held buzzed with anticipation. Educators, business leaders, and students had gathered to witness the unveiling of the new initiative—a program designed to empower people to redefine success, to embrace risk, and to grow through failure.

Aniket stood off to the side of the stage, his heart pounding as he watched Sahil step up to the microphone. Sahil's presence commanded attention, and as he began to speak, the room fell into a reverent hush.

"Thank you all for being here," Sahil began, his voice steady and filled with passion. "Today, we are talking about change. Not just in education or business, but in the way we think about success, about life itself."

Aniket felt a surge of pride as Sahil's words rippled through the crowd. This was what they had worked for. This was why they had faced the challenges and pushed past the doubts.

"For too long, we've been told that success is about perfection," Sahil continued. "But true success is about growth. It's about resilience. It's about the courage to take risks, to embrace failure, to learn and evolve."

A murmur of agreement swept through the room. Aniket felt his heart swell with emotion, knowing that the message they were sharing was resonating.

"We've created something that challenges the status quo," Sahil said. "A program that empowers people to see success not as a final destination, but as a continuous journey of becoming."

The applause was thunderous, and as Sahil stepped aside, Aniket took his place at the podium. His heart pounded with a mix of nerves and excitement, but as he began to speak, he felt the words come naturally.

"Together, we are redefining success," Aniket said, his voice strong. "We are building something that challenges the old ways of thinking—something that empowers people to grow, to evolve, to make a real difference."

The standing ovation that followed was overwhelming. As Aniket and Sahil stood side by side on that stage, they knew they had achieved something far greater than they had ever imagined.

Because this wasn't just about building a business. It was about creating a legacy—one step, one failure, one success at a time.

Epilogue: The Meaning of Success

The sun dipped below the horizon, casting a warm, amber glow over the landscape as evening descended. The soft rustling of leaves and distant chirping of crickets created a soothing melody in the air. Aniket and Sahil sat on a bench in the garden of the retreat center they had recently opened. The center had become a sanctuary for people seeking to rediscover themselves—to learn, to grow, and to redefine their lives. The crisp air carried the faint scent of pine, and with it, the promise of a peaceful night.

They had come a long way since their early days of chasing after conventional success, their journey marked by personal transformation and a shared vision. Together, they had built something extraordinary—something that had touched countless lives. But despite all they had achieved, both knew that their journey was far from over. As they sat side by side, watching the sky shift from gold to deep blue, there was a quiet contentment, a sense of fulfilment that could only come from knowing they had made a lasting difference.

Aniket leaned back, his eyes wandering over the sprawling grounds of the retreat. The softly lit paths, the silhouettes of people gathered under trees, talking, laughing, and sharing their stories, all filled him with a deep sense of peace. This place had become a reflection of their shared values—a space for exploration, for embracing failure, and for discovering new possibilities.

"It's beautiful, isn't it?" Sahil's voice broke the stillness, soft yet filled with awe. His words carried the same quiet reverence that Aniket felt.

Aniket nodded, his gaze lingering on a group of young people laughing under the shade of a tree, their joy carried by the breeze. "It is. It's everything we envisioned, and more."

Sahil smiled; his eyes thoughtful. "We've come a long way, haven't we? From those days of obsessing over grades, striving for perfection... to this. It's incredible how much we've learned, how much we've grown."

Aniket sighed, feeling the depth of Sahil's words resonate in his heart. "Yes, we have. But it's not just about what we've built; it's about who we've become. I used to think success was about getting everything right—never failing, always achieving. Now I know it's about so much more than that."

Sahil nodded, his eyes fixed on the horizon, as if seeing beyond what was visible. "It's about the journey—the growth that happens when we're willing to take risks, to stumble, and to keep moving forward despite the setbacks. Success isn't about avoiding failure; it's about embracing it as part of the process."

Aniket felt his throat tighten with emotion, the truth of Sahil's words sinking deeper than ever before. "I was so afraid of failure for so long. I thought that making mistakes meant I wasn't good enough. But now I see that failure isn't the opposite of success. It's a necessary step along the way. Without it, we never really learn, we never really grow."

Sahil glanced at him, his eyes filled with understanding and pride. "We've both come so far. We've faced our fears, embraced our failures, and in doing so, we've created something that challenges the old ways of thinking—something that shows people success isn't about what you achieve, but about who you become and the impact you make."

Aniket smiled, feeling the weight of those words lift him. "And the people we've helped along the way—showing them that their worth isn't tied to their accomplishments, but to their willingness to explore, to try, to fail. We've built something that matters."

Sahil leaned back, looking up at the first stars appearing in the twilight. "Success isn't about titles, degrees, or wealth. It's about living a life aligned with who you truly are—your values, your passions, your purpose."

Aniket nodded, remembering the days when he believed his value was measured by his achievements and his ability to meet others' expectations. "I spent so many years chasing other people's definitions of success. I thought if I did everything right, I'd finally feel fulfilled. But real success is about finding your own path, about defining success on your terms."

Sahil's voice was filled with quiet wisdom, the kind that comes from hard-earned experience. "That's exactly what we've been trying to teach here. It's okay to fail. It's okay to struggle. It's okay to be imperfect. Those are the things that shape us, that make us stronger. That's where the real growth happens."

Tears stung the corners of Aniket's eyes as he reflected on their shared journey. "We've created a space where people can come to explore their potential, take risks, fail, and grow. A place where they can redefine what success means to them—where they can find their own purpose, their own truth."

Sahil's smile softened. "We've built a new way of thinking—one that values experience over achievement, growth over perfection, and courage over certainty."

The night was falling gently around them, and the retreat's guests continued to walk the paths, their conversations and laughter a quiet reminder of the lives being touched, the changes being made.

"And it's not just about professional success," Sahil said after a moment, his voice thoughtful. "It's about success in all aspects of life. In relationships, in personal growth, in the choices we make every day. It's about living a life that feels meaningful, that's aligned with who you truly are."

Aniket's heart swelled with the truth of his friend's words. "I've seen so many people who have everything—money, titles, status—but who still feel empty, like something is missing."

Sahil's gaze was steady, filled with a quiet resolve. "That's because real success isn't about what you have, it's about who you are. It's about the quality of your relationships, the depth of your experiences, and how authentic you are in the way you live your life."

Aniket felt a profound sense of peace, a clarity that had eluded him for so long. "That's what we're here to teach. That it's okay to take risks, to struggle, to fail. Because those are the moments where life truly happens, where we grow into who we're meant to be."

Sahil's eyes softened with affection. "You've come so far, Aniket. You've learned the real meaning of success, of failure, and of growth. And now, you're helping others do the same—helping them find their own paths."

Aniket was filled with gratitude. "We're all on our own journeys, trying to figure out what it means to live a fulfilling life. The greatest lesson is that there's no one way to be successful. It's about finding your own way, your own truth."

Sahil looked out at the stars that now dotted the sky. "And having the courage to follow that path, no matter the risks, no matter the failures."

They sat in companionable silence for a while, the night wrapping around them like a comforting blanket. The peace of the evening settled into their bones, the quiet murmur of voices in the distance a reminder of the lives they had touched, the legacy they were building.

Eventually, Sahil spoke again, his voice low and reflective. "We've learned that success isn't measured by traditional markers. It's about living authentically—about courage, growth, and the pursuit of something bigger than ourselves."

Aniket's heart swelled. "It's about building a life that's meaningful—full of rich experiences, deep relationships, and constant growth."

As they sat together in the retreat they had built from their shared dreams, their friendship and vision stronger than ever, they knew that this was only the beginning. There were still so many paths to explore, so many lessons to learn, and so many lives to touch.

And as the stars continued to brighten the night sky, Aniket and Sahil, two dreamers who had redefined success on their own terms, were ready for whatever came next.

Because they weren't just building a retreat, a business, or even a model for success. They were building a legacy—one step, one failure, and one success at a time.

Life, after all, is a continuous journey, whether you're a first-bencher or a last-bencher.

And they were ready for it.

End.

www.ingramcontent.com/pod-product-compliance
Lightning Source LLC
Chambersburg PA
CBHW021532150726
47990CB00006B/2206